LIGHT ON FIRE

LIGHT ON FIRE

Waking Up to Divine Love

AEDAMAR KIRRANE

HAY HOUSE

Carlsbad, California • New York City
London • Sydney • New Delhi

Published in the United Kingdom by:
Hay House UK Ltd, The Sixth Floor, Watson House,
54 Baker Street, London W1U 7BU
Tel: +44 (0)20 3927 7290; Fax: +44 (0)20 3927 7291; www.hayhouse.co.uk

Published in the United States of America by:
Hay House Inc., PO Box 5100, Carlsbad, CA 92018-5100
Tel: (1) 760 431 7695 or (800) 654 5126
Fax: (1) 760 431 6948 or (800) 650 5115; www.hayhouse.com

Published in Australia by:
Hay House Australia Pty Ltd, 18/36 Ralph St, Alexandria NSW 2015
Tel: (61) 2 9669 4299; Fax: (61) 2 9669 4144; www.hayhouse.com.au

Published in India by:
Hay House Publishers India, Muskaan Complex,
Plot No.3, B-2, Vasant Kunj, New Delhi 110 070
Tel: (91) 11 4176 1620; Fax: (91) 11 4176 1630; www.hayhouse.co.in

A catalogue record for this book is available from the British Library.

Tradepaper ISBN: 978-1-78817-474-9
E-book ISBN: 978-1-78817-480-0
Audiobook ISBN: 978-1-78817-593-7

Interior illustrations: Allison Cooke

Printed and bound by CPI Group (UK) Ltd, Croydon CR0 4YY

This book is dedicated to the memory of my beloved parents, Máire and Séamus Kirrane – I am forever grateful for their love and devotion. My mother's bold, passionate and visionary approach to life was inspirational; a living lesson in what it takes to live one's truth. My father's fathomless love and his deep, quiet wisdom was always my safe harbour. I thank you for inspiring me to live my best life. I love you, and I miss you both, every day.

'I AM the Annunciation of Love.
Announce my Love.'
JESUS[*]

CONTENTS

PART II: REPLACING THE NARRATIVE OF SEPARATION WITH A NARRATIVE OF LOVE

A PATH OF GOLD

'I have laid before you a Path of Gold.
Take my hand and let me guide you on the Way.
I know the Way because I AM The Way.'
JESUS

The year 2020 had barely begun when our social, political and cultural zeitgeist exploded with an inner necessity for radical and transformational change. COVID-19 brought the world to a halt and it brought us face to face with the questions we are usually too busy to ask. Questions about how we live and about whether our life is aligned with our truth; whether our work is aligned with our soul; and whether we have found our true calling in life. As COVID-19 multiplied exponentially and uncontrollably across the globe, the world went into lockdown and an uncanny hush descended that opened up a liminal space for this much-needed reflection and self-questioning.

Into the quiet of this liminal space George Floyd gasped his last words. Mr Floyd's casual, racist murder triggered shock waves through a public consciousness by then ripe for asking the big questions. It catapulted us into a deeper and more urgent questioning of who we are as a species, of how we live, and of how we treat each other.

Righteous rage erupted across the globe, inspiring people to take to the streets in protest that Black Lives Matter. The powerful emotion expressed in these protest marches went beyond the BLM movement to a righteous rage at the state of humanity itself, at ourselves and at how we live, at what we tolerate, and at all that we ignore so that our lives of privilege can go on without disruption. It became a righteous rage at the stark reality that, on the only planet in our galaxy that can sustain life, we choose to kill each other.

In the blink of an eye humanity reached breaking point – as if a valve had exploded in the collective psyche, propelling us into a global awakening. Each of us now urgently wanting to know how to live better lives, how to be our best self so that others can be their best self too, how to be a light of love in the world, and how to live authentically with deep meaning and higher purpose. The inextricable connection between all of our lives was laid bare and prompted within us a palpable and urgent desire to live in a better way, and to learn how to contribute to the healing of the world that is so desperately needed at this time.

The year 2020 marks a line in the sand for humanity. Clearly, we are in an evolutionary moment of seismic change, and if we do not fix things now, there may well be nothing at all to fix in the future. We know we cannot go on any longer living in this broken and dysfunctional way. There is too much suffering, too much pain, too much brokenness. We must find a new and a better way forwards.

This new way forwards is a radical and fundamental transformation of our consciousness. Such a transformation is traditionally called an awakening – it is a shift to a higher level of consciousness and an awakening to a power greater than ourselves. By undergoing our spiritual awakening, we allow ourselves to be guided by the higher power of God in order to become the best and truest version of ourselves, to live our best life with deep meaning and higher purpose, and to live with profound and sacred concern for everyone else on the planet and for the planet itself. When we do wake up in this way, we discover that the whole meaning and purpose of life is in fact to awaken to our truth as beings of love belonging to love itself. Awakening is an entirely natural life event from which we have become estranged – with disastrous consequence.

The way forwards does not lie only with governments and world leaders; rather it lies with each of us, individually committing to this transformation in our own lives. Committing to a transformation of the consciousness that informs how we live individually and collectively and that, most especially, informs how we treat this beautiful planet we should feel blessed to live on but which instead we desecrate and destroy.

It becomes imperative, therefore, to identify the consciousness from which we are currently operating – the one that produces this broken and dysfunctional world – and to identify the higher consciousness from which we need to be operating if we are to live our best lives. Our current consciousness – the one we have been operating from for the past 2,500 years in the West – is rational-intellectual consciousness. The consciousness we need to be operating from instead is spiritual consciousness.

Since the time of Socrates, Plato and Aristotle, the dominant consciousness of Western culture has increasingly been the intellectual-scientific-egoic consciousness that first emerged for humanity between 800–200BCE and culminated in the Enlightenment of the 17th and 18th centuries. The phenomenal gifts of the intellect are undeniable and have allowed for unimagined progress in nearly every walk of life – although not for everybody. What has become manifestly evident, however, is that the better life we long for, individually and collectively, simply cannot be achieved at the current level of consciousness. If it could, it would surely have come about by now.

When reasoning first emerged, the thinkers and philosophers of the day wrongly determined that reason had come to *replace* all that had gone before it. Blinded by the brilliance of reason, beside which spirit looked primitive, they failed to appreciate that the gift of reason was an evolutionary unfolding designed to complement our natural spirituality rather than to supplant it. Our newly rational consciousness ought to have been integrated with our pre-existing spiritual consciousness, but was instead allowed to replace it. We thought we could live on the track of reason alone; but our rationally oriented, materialistic, secular, broken and dysfunctional culture and civilization gives the lie to that idea.

Aristotle's famous definition of humans as 'rational animals' captures perfectly the wholesale elevation of intellect over spirituality.

It has become all too obvious, from the broken state of our lives and our world, that intellectual consciousness is not designed to facilitate higher living from a place of authenticity, truth and love. The intellect operates through theory, ideas, logic and rational analysis; and while these are of course magnificent tools for meaning-making and understanding, they do not of themselves give us the better world we long for. Something more is needed in order to make our ideas of a better world actionable. That something 'more' is mature spiritual consciousness. The leavening agent of spiritual consciousness is critical for rounding out the proper functioning of reason, and this is the consciousness we urgently need to shift into if we are to become our best selves and to create a better world for all.

Many of us are struggling with a fundamental loss of meaning in our lives, sensing that there must be a better way than this; intuiting that there could be so much more to life if we just knew how to access it. We perceive that our life is off track; that we are stuck and we cannot find our purpose. We feel disconnected from ourselves, each other, nature and from the higher power. These feelings stem from the fact that we are trying to live better lives, and trying to find higher meaning and purpose, with either intellectual, psychological or egoic consciousness, or with underdeveloped spiritual consciousness – neither of which can provide the level of meaning we crave.

Equally, at the global level, behind the multiple crises of our time, spanning climate destruction, war, poverty, injustice, inequality, racism, refugee crises, authoritarianism and so many more catastrophes, there also lies this singular spiritual crisis: that our natural spirituality has been repressed, suppressed and oppressed in favour of leading with reason; so much so that we have forgotten how to wake up to our higher selves.

The good news is that, despite these disastrous historic mis-steps, our natural spirituality did not die off as some unnecessary evolutionary residuum. It lives on in us, as a wholly natural part of who we are, quietly seeking healthy, authentic expression, and pushing us towards our spiritual awakening even though we no longer understand what that is.

In 2015, the tectonic plates of my own life shifted when I began to experience a spontaneous spiritual awakening. I was not on a spiritual path, and I did not understand what was happening to me, but seismic change nonetheless introduced itself into my life.

Jesus began to come to me, in sacred fire, during meditation, speaking the most tender love into my heart, and transforming me utterly within the depths of my being: *Hold me in your heart, as I hold you in mine. You are my own daughter of love; I AM you and you are me. We are one. The light of Christ is in you – go set fire to the world.*

My daily meditations became indescribably holy, Jesus and God often lifting my spirit out of my body and bringing me into the blazing light of their love – dissolving my finitude, transfiguring me to light, so that I merged one with One in the ecstatic light of their love: *Tell my friends you have seen the light and that the light is love.* Almost every day, for about two years, I had the most sacred, ineffable, indescribably beautiful mystical experiences during meditation.

Part One: Opening to the Mystic

Part One of this book will share my lived experience of this extraordinary awakening, which brought me out of this world and into rapturous union with God and with Jesus. I became light, I became love, I became peace, I became joy. My whole being was transfigured, so that I knew myself in my original creation in the mind of God as a child of the light and as a child of love. And at the same time, I also came to know every single other person on Earth, equally, at their core, as a child of the light and as a child of love.

My heart, my mind and my soul exploded in a fire of divine love, and my whole life transformed. I learned how it is that we come from love, and that we return to love; and for some reason I have been allowed to experience the exquisite return to love before I die. I see now, with new eyes and with a new heart, that Life itself is a gift of love that, tragically, we have failed to understand. In return for Jesus gifting me this exquisite awakening to divine love, I have been asked to share my story. This book is my story.

Part of the story includes my struggle to accept this mystic gift; how I grappled with the implications for my life, and how, before anything else, I had to consider the possibility that I may have been going mad. Or, if I was sane, was I prepared to sacrifice my own hard-won plans in life to follow this difficult and highly unusual call? There were struggles in every direction, but the biggest struggle of all was when Jesus asked me to write this book. Every cell in my body resisted.

I admit that finding the courage to respond to this call and to write this book has been the most difficult yet rewarding challenge of my life. I accepted that the mystic must always come back to the community and share what she has experienced and learned. Mystics are essentially messengers and so I have written this book as a messenger of love for my beloved Mother-Father God, for Jesus, Mary Magdalene, Mother Mary and for anyone who longs to awaken but has not known how to do so.

PART TWO: REPLACING THE NARRATIVE OF SEPARATION WITH A NARRATIVE OF LOVE

Part Two of the book then moves beyond my own personal story into the wider question of why the entire context of our privileged Western life is silent about even the possibility of any of us having this awakening experience. Why there is a black hole where there should be appropriate teaching, wisdom and guidance around this incredible life event. Why my Catholic religion – and indeed every other Western faith – offers no guidance on the magnificent experience of embodied awakening as a natural life event for lay people. My determination to understand what was happening to me, and to find out why there was no framing context for it in my life, religion or culture, catapulted me into five years of private research. My studies led me to explore the history of Western civilization, the history of Christianity, mysticism and mystical theology across all the traditions, in order to find out what has gone so wrong with our culture that it neglects and ignores this most important phase of our human development.

TO DEMYSTIFY AND NORMALIZE SPIRITUAL AWAKENING

The central insight that this book offers – the one thing that I truly hope you will take away with you, and that has the potential to change your life – is the insight that awakening is a wholly natural and normal life event. It is something that is meant to begin happening for each of us in early middle age. We should expect it to happen, as naturally as we expect puberty, menstruation and the menopause to happen to us on the physical-biological plane. My deepest hope is that this book will help demystify spiritual awakening and restore it to its natural place as a critical milestone on our journey through life.

The second crucial insight this book offers is that we are all called to be mystics. We are designed to wake up. We are meant to wake up. And we need to wake up. The whole meaning and purpose of life is for us to wake up to the truth of who we are – beings of light in the light, and beings of love in love. Yet, we have become so estranged from the wisdom, the energetics and the dynamics of awakening that we don't even know how it works anymore. We no longer understand the signs of it trying to unfold as a natural life event, and therefore we unwittingly block it from happening.

But our body, our mind and our soul instinctively know how to let this transformation of consciousness happen, and so our job is to learn how to unblock the blocks. We need to re-educate ourselves about this phenomenal and natural life process. We need to re-learn how to let our awakening happen. We need to re-embrace the sacred and commit to re-spiritualizing our lives. We need to retrieve what was lost in order to come into our truth, to save ourselves, our species and our planet at this darkest time in human history.

THE NARRATIVE OF SEPARATION THAT UNDERLIES WESTERN CIVILIZATION

From my years of research and reflection I discovered that the root cause of all of our suffering today, both individually and collectively, is located precisely in that early rupture between reason and spirit I mentioned earlier. This foundational rupture then led to a domino effect of further ruptures between God and humanity; humanity and nature; science and religion; spirit and matter; masculine and feminine; human and human; and mind and body. All of this inscribed a destructive narrative of separation into the mind, the psyche and the soul of Western humanity. It is precisely this mindset of separation and division that underlies all the disconnection, inequality and injustice that infects our world today. In understanding how things went wrong we can work towards replacing the separated mind of Western culture with a healing mindset of oneness in love. Only then will we be able to flourish in love as we are uniquely designed to do.

THE SPIRITUAL FAILURE OF CHRISTIANITY

Part Two will also share my insights into some of what has gone wrong for Christianity: why it has failed in its moral and spiritual leadership, and how the story of the fall, and the doctrine of original sin, compounded the ruptures between God and humanity, and between reason and spirit. We often hear representatives of all the Western faiths arguing that the spiritual hunger, and the spiritual vacuum, that exists in our culture today is the consequence of people leaving organized religion. But I think those representatives fundamentally misunderstand the situation. People have left organized religion precisely *because* the Church was not responding to our deep and innate longing for transformative spiritual *experience*.

One of the key mis-steps by Christianity, for example, was to exclude meditation and mysticism from the mainstream religious practice of lay people. These are central features of all Eastern religions and without them the Christian Church inevitably imposed a spiritual glass ceiling on what people could experience in the ordinary course of their Christian faith. Christianity settled for teaching an immature, superficial spirituality that was unlikely to bring people into an embodied, mystical relationship with God as part and parcel of their everyday lives.

There is a deep confusion that many Christians wrestle with today: how to be a Christian when our Church is so broken? In grappling with this question myself, while writing this book, I finally understood that Jesus was not calling on me or anybody else to convert to, or to revert to, Christianity but is instead calling for Christianity itself to convert to the religion of love it was always meant to be. We *need* a New Christianity of Love.

THE PATH OF GOLD: A GUIDE TO AWAKENING

Chapter 15 then shares the guide that I have created for others who long to awaken and to experience this transformation of consciousness in their own lives. It began as a personal project to plot the milestones of my own awakening but, in the end, I realized that the inner dynamics, energetics and milestones of my own awakening had universal application and were, in fact, the archetypal or developmental milestones of every awakening.

This guide provides a master framework of the seven stages of awakening that I have identified from my own experience. It begins by listing the signs of spiritual dis-ease that signal our awakening is trying to unfold, and it shares the spiritual tools and practices necessary to engage meaningfully with them. It then offers help for navigating the golden path to love through the seven stages of awakening.

In offering a spiritual map of the awakening process, the guide will help you to engage meaningfully with your awakening as a natural life event. It is the guide I wish I had when I was haphazardly walking through my own sacred awakening, with almost no understanding of what was happening to me and grappling in the moment with powerful spiritual, energetic and mystical experiences.

A MESSAGE OF HOPE

The book ends with hope, and with a profound conviction that the higher consciousness that is trying to come through at this time will prevail. That our misunderstanding of the meaning and purpose of life can be undone by each of us allowing our consciousness to be transformed into a mystical consciousness of love. The hope for ourselves, our species and our planet lies in our willingness to surrender to our own individual awakening.

We do not have time to wait for world leaders or our churches to catch up with what is needed; instead we must take the lead ourselves. Global awakening depends on each of us taking responsibility for our own individual awakening. It is only by awakening that we will heal and transform our lives and contribute to the healing and transformation of the whole world.

I thank you from my heart for choosing this book and I hope that it will serve you well. I hope that it will ignite, inspire and support your own beautiful experience of awakening to divine love.

With love and joy,

Aedamar xoxo

> '*Burn in the fire of my Love, as*
> *I burn in the fire of your love for me.*
>
> *Let me burn away everything in you that is not me,*
> *So that I may be you, and you may be me.*
>
> *I AM you and you are me.*
> *Together we are One in the Fire of Love.*'
>
> JESUS

~

PRELIMINARY NOTES ON GOD AND MYSTICISM

'I AM Peace, I AM Joy, I AM Stillness, I AM Love.'
Voice of God[†]

We are going to be speaking a lot about God and mysticism in this book, so it may be helpful to say a few things about my understanding of these terms at the outset.

1. WHAT IS GOD?

God is the name we give to the highest power. We must move beyond the childish and patriarchal notion of God as 'a masculine being in the sky'. Whatever God is, God is not a being, and nor does it have a gender. God is not a being because God is Being itself. A being is finite, whereas God is infinite. God as Being is also pure intelligence which has the character

---

† All quotes from God were spoken to Aedamar in meditation except where otherwise indicated.

of love. These divine identities of being, intelligence and love are interchangeable names for God: God is being, God is intelligence and God is love.

There are many names for what we call God, but there is only one God. There are many religions and spiritual systems but still there is only one God. Some of the names we are familiar with for God are: Spirit, the One, the All, Life, Being, Intellect, Pure Mind, Energy, Consciousness. But they are all different names for the same thing – the creative power of Life. In the 13th century, Meister Eckhart prayed to God 'to rid him of God', meaning he wanted to be free of any concept of God in order to access the purity of what God is, beyond and above all language and thought.

There are two schools of thought when it comes to describing God: cataphatic and apophatic. Cataphatic thought offers ever more abundant descriptions in its attempts to express the infinite, eternal and abundant goodness of God. Apophatic thought, on the other hand, argues that God is beyond all possible language, description and knowing, and therefore adopts a position of negating anything that might purport to be a description of God. The apophatic school prefer to say all the things that God is *not*.

In this book I will offer a mix of the two, drawing from mystics and philosophers who have sought to describe God over the millennia. 'God is that beyond which nothing greater can be conceived,' wrote St Anselm in the 11th century. God is the Infinite, the All. God is All-benevolent, All-loving, All-knowing,

Unchanging and Unchangeable. God Self-created out of nothing, God is the Creator of All without itself being created. According to Aristotle, God is the unmoved first mover.

God is the circumference of the circle and its centre. God is the Container and the contained; the Creator and the created. God is all there is. Everything is in God and God is in everything. Nothing exists outside God. God is unknowable. God is greater than anything that could ever be said of God. God is indescribable. God is pure no-thing-ness. Language cannot reach the level needed to describe God. God can only be reached in silence and unknowing. In God there is no difference, division or separation. In God all is joined in one peaceful, harmonious whole. God is the Logos, or the Divine Principle of Life. God is the Creative Principle. God is Pure Intelligence, or the Intellectual Principle. God is Pure Being. God is Love. God is transcendent. God is immanent. And all of these things are paradoxically true of God.

2. How Can We Know God?

The only way to know God is to have a lived experience of God. What does that mean? I hope this book will answer that question for you.

3. What Is a Mystic?

At its most basic, a mystic is someone who has had the felt or lived experience of knowing the joyous connection of all to All;

of seeing, feeling and knowing, with the whole of their body, mind and spirit, that everything is connected in a meaningful whole. A mystic is someone who then tries to live this truth in their everyday life.

The mystical scholar Caroline Spurgeon defines mystics as those who 'all alike agree... in one passionate assertion... that unity underlies diversity'. She says that the 'basic fact of mysticism... [is] founded on an intuitive or experienced conviction of unity, of oneness, of alikeness in all things.'[‡]

4. WHAT IS A MYSTICAL EXPERIENCE?

A mystical experience can span a broad spectrum of events, from a profound knowing of God in the soul, to being brought out of one's body and into sacred union with the divine, which has been described since the time of Plato as: *unio mystica*. This book shares descriptions of each stage of my mystical experience from profound inner knowing, to union with God as the blazing light of love.

> *'Let your words be like roses blossoming*
> *on my crown of thorns.'*
>
> JESUS

~

[‡] Spurgeon, Caroline, F.E., *Mysticism in English Literature*. The Echo Library, Middlesex (first published Cambridge: Cambridge University Press, 1913; reprinted, 2006)

PART I

~

OPENING
TO THE
MYSTIC

I

I am laughter, I am joy
I am tears, I am suffering
I do not belong here, or there –
I belong in-between.

II

I move between two worlds
Singing the Song of Love.

III

I am courage, I am fear
I am hope, I am hopelessness
I am not Love, I am Love
I am nothing, I am everything.

IV

All that I do, I am,
I am The I AM.
I AM you. You are Me
We are One.

AEDAMAR

CHAPTER 1

IN THE WOMB
OF CHRIST

'I hold you in the womb of my Love,
As you hold me in the womb of your love.
Hold me as your own creation of Love, and
Birth me out into the world, so all will know that
I AM Nothing but Love.'
JESUS

On Christmas Day 2014, my completely ordinary life as a 46-year-old mother, wife, former lawyer, and now mature student of philosophy and English, took a dramatic, unprecedented and extraordinary turn.

I do admit to some peculiarities about myself and about how I experienced life – things that I had never understood, such as spontaneous altered states of consciousness; strange moods during which I became detached from ordinary reality yet was able to function normally. I lived with a profound intuition that I did not belong on Earth, or to humanity, and I had a lifelong sense that I was lost at a primordial level. I lived with an urgent feeling that I was searching for something vast and cosmic without knowing what it was, and I had spent my life seeking meaning that I could not find. I lived with a perception that I existed somehow 'between two worlds' without ever understanding what that meant. These feelings were with me from my earliest memories and I shared them with no one because I could not understand, describe or explain any of it.

Nonetheless, thus far in my life, I had always stayed in my body and had a very arm's-length relationship with God – but not for much longer. My unusual experiences were about to take centre stage in my life and catapult me into the sacred experience of mystical union with God, which gave me a whole new understanding of myself, humanity, nature, life and God.

On that fateful Christmas Day, my huge Irish family – five sisters, one brother, plus our spouses and children, making almost 40 in total – was gathered for Christmas dinner in my eldest sister's home. Our father had recently passed away. We were all heartbroken, and our grief was still very raw. A group of us were sitting by the fire chatting when someone mentioned Séan Boylan. I had never heard of Séan before, but as people chatted about how he was a famous Gaelic football manager and a gifted herbalist with a herbal clinic in County Meath, the strangest thing happened inside my head. Crystal clear and full of authority, my voice spontaneously spoke to me – as if it had suddenly acquired a will of its own. Silently, but very firmly, it said, *That's the place for me!*

How strange. How could I possibly say this to myself with such – or any – authority, when I had never heard of Séan's clinic before? I was intrigued. The only explanation I could think of was that Séan might be able to help with the unexplained partial deafness in my left ear that had developed in 2012, and that modern medicine had said could not be reversed.

Only once before in my life had a voice, or my voice, spoken spontaneously inside my head. It had happened seven years previously, in 2007, when I was 39 and on summer holidays with my own small family: my husband and our two children, then aged five and three. We were staying on the Skellig Coast of Valentia Island in the wild and majestic west of Ireland. It has always been the pleasure of my soul to walk alone in nature – the more remote, barren and isolated, the better. One evening, as the sun was setting, I was walking along the Atlantic coastline, enjoying the supernatural beauty of this ancient landscape. I looked out to the Skellig rocks, imagining the 6th-century Christian monks living their ascetic lives of prayer on those black stony cliffs that erupt almost biblically up out of the Atlantic Ocean. As I walked, that strange but familiar feeling of detachment began to come over me.

It came on imperceptibly as usual, giving me a gradual sense of becoming estranged from ordinary life; making me feel as if I had been switched onto a different wavelength and a crucial gap had inserted itself between me and the workings of the ordinary world. Things no longer made sense in those moods. I felt as if I were floating in between places, such that I had left the world but had not actually arrived anywhere else. I was hovering between two states in every way. In these moods, the ordinary world lost its meaning, it became pointless, and nothing seemed real or important anymore. I became an onlooker on life, as if I were now somehow *outside* of life and watching it from a distance.

I was always passive in these experiences; I would never have been able to make it happen by myself – I would not have known how. The moods usually ended as imperceptibly as they began, delivering me seamlessly back to ordinary awareness. I never told a living soul about these experiences. They were my own strange private affair.

It was exactly this mood that I felt coming over me that August evening as I walked along the Atlantic coastline. Only this time, the experience took a markedly different turn from usual.

My walk took me as far as the harbour at Glanleam, which is a quaint little cove, accessed by a winding path down the side of a steep hill. There is a short pier at which only a small number of fishing boats can moor. I have always felt a deep connection to harbours, and I chose the name Cuan for my son, which is the Irish word for 'harbour or place of safety'.

As I reached the shoreline, my feeling of detachment accelerated dramatically in a way that I had never experienced before. I became completely disconnected from the beach, the sea, the world, and even from my own self. I had to stop walking. Powerful energy was building inside me and all around me.

Yet, despite the strangeness, I was not at all frightened because there was an amazing sense of beauty and calm in what was happening. As I stood there, at the edge of the Atlantic, the feeling developed exponentially so that I lost all awareness of my physical self and the physical world around me. I began to feel my entire self being lifted wholly out of ordinary existence, out of life, out of the world. As this happened, I was filled with supernatural calm and I felt myself being carried into a place of profound peace. It was the most beautiful thing that had ever happened to me in my entire life.

I felt as if I were now floating in a place of supreme peace beyond the confines of the world, in a place where not even the possibility of conflict could enter. It was a place of pure oneness. I did not feel my spirit to have left my body, which later became my daily experience; rather, my whole being seemed to be involved in the experience, as if maybe I had died without realizing it. It instilled in me the most beautiful, sublime, peaceful feeling of all being very well, and I felt amazing in a way that would be impossible to recreate in ordinary life. It was literally out of this world. My fullest experience was of being in a beautiful place of stillness and peace. Everything else – the beach, the mountains, the world, my own physical self – faded completely from my awareness, essentially into non-existence.

I felt as if I had been taken wholly and completely, in my whole being, into peace itself.

7

After a while the strange and beautiful experience began to end. My guess afterwards was that it had lasted about 45 minutes. It is difficult to explain how it ended. The feeling of extreme detachment and deep peace was slowly ebbing, and this world was coming back into focus. Or maybe it would be better to describe it as being delivered back to 'this world' from that other 'place'. A helpful analogy at the physical level might be the thought of being numbed at the dentist. When the numbness starts to fade, feeling slowly returns. It was something like that, but at the level of the mind.

Just as I had had no control over the entry into this state, I had no control over emerging from it either – but I was deeply upset for it to be ending. I wanted it to last forever. No life experience anyone could ever have in ordinary consciousness could come close to the peace, serenity and stillness I had just experienced. In the past, it had never bothered me when the moods ended; I simply got back into the regular gear of life and kept going as if nothing had happened.

But this time, it was completely different.

I was desperate, almost frantic, to try to hold onto something of the experience. If I could not stay in that place of peace forever, then at the very least I wanted to bring something of it back with me. I cast my eyes around, desperately looking to the ocean, the beach, the mountains for help, wanting to capture something of it before it dissipated entirely, like air into air, and I would find myself wondering if it had even really happened. It occurred to me to try to feel or imagine my way back into the energy of the experience, just as you might try to rekindle a dream before fully waking up. As I tried to do that, I heard my inner voice spontaneously asking the question: *What would you do if you could stay in this feeling forever?* I have no idea how I came to ask such a question, but I had an incredibly deep conviction, which I felt with every cell of my body, that if I could only discover what it would take to live in that place of peace forever, I would devote my entire life to doing that thing, whatever it might be.

Before I had even begun, however, to consider what it might take to be able to live in this place of peace forever, before any ideas had formed in my mind, and with no forethought whatsoever, I suddenly heard a voice – or my own voice (I cannot say which) – inside my head, speaking spontaneously, crystal clear, and with great majesty. With a will of its own, and with profound energetic vibration, the voice replied with these strange words: *I would walk into that mountainside and re-enter the womb of Christ.*

I was dumbfounded.

The words unleashed powerful feelings in me. It was the most majestic sentence I had ever heard uttered. But where had it come from? I had formed no intention to speak, never mind say such a sentence. I had never heard the phrase 'the womb of Christ' before. I looked over at the mountain just beyond the harbour, knowing somehow that that was the mountainside to which the words were referring. As I looked at it, an image formed in my mind of me laying myself flat, arms outstretched, face down, on the mountainside. I visualized my body sinking into the earth and melding with it, becoming one with it, becoming earth. And I knew, somehow, that that was how I would re-enter the womb of Christ. This powerful image richly and perfectly answered the intensity of my desire for the experience to continue forever. If I had had the slightest intuition that laying my body down on the earth in that way could cause all this to happen, I would have done it immediately, but I knew it would not.

I did, however, now know the *feeling* of what it would be like to stay in the experience of peace forever. It would be like being dead. It would be like resting forever in blissful and eternal peace in the *womb of Christ*.

It then dawned on me that the entire event had been a holy experience. I felt blessed – knowing something sacred had occurred, but not understanding what, how or why. I was in a state of awe, unable to think and overwhelmed by the sheer beauty of it all. Aristotle wrote that, 'All knowing, begins in wonder,' and I was now experiencing *pure* wonder – the knowing would take a lot longer.

When I knew that the experience was definitely coming to an end and that I was coming back to my full senses and awareness, I was incredibly sad. I was also in a state of shock. This world seemed completely insignificant by comparison with where I had been. I kept asking myself, *What just happened?*, but I had no answer. The whole thing completely transcended human explanation. There was nothing in my life experience to date that even tentatively touched on giving me an insight into what had just happened. The one conclusion I reached was that to be home in the *womb of Christ* as suggested, one would need to be dead. At some very deep level, I sensed that the return to the *womb of Christ* must represent the final homecoming to heaven, the final resting place.

My mind was full of the strangeness and the beauty of the experience, and of knowing that I had lived through something astonishing that I could not understand.

It was now after 10 p.m., the sun had set, and I knew I had to return to the holiday house. I walked slowly and with great reluctance because every step was drawing me further back into what I guessed was now to be the 'old life', the life before this experience had occurred. This had been a milestone, a crossing point, a threshold experience in my life, yet I had no idea what it meant. I was changed utterly, but I did not know how.

Back at the house, I could not hide from my husband that something very peculiar had happened to me. I was still quite out of it, and I could not and did not want to engage properly with him. Even the quiet act of speaking seemed loud, grating and crass. I felt as if my mind were plugged into a different wavelength and I had no interest in re-establishing full communication with this realm. My husband had known nothing of my secret moods and my unusual feelings – no one did. Normally I kept my musings and uncommon experiences to myself, but this time I could not hide my odd state, and so I did my best to tell him something of what had happened on my walk. My husband has no natural interest in things like this, so he did not try to delve into what I could not explain.

The following morning when I awoke, the mood had lifted and I was 'back to normal' but shaken. Poetry seemed the only appropriate response, so over the next few days I wrote this poem about the experience:

Evening at Glanleam Harbour

My body is open,
A weight coddles my mind,
The island mountains, filled with turf, talk to me
But I struggle to understand what they say.

The waters of the Womb lap at the shoreline.
The first birth tearing us from our Maker,
And we repeat that scream on each tide.

The Thought which created us left a flicker in us, a spark.

A fire is now building inside me,
Its flames cleanse and anoint for a holy moment;
I then hurl myself into the mountainside
And re-enter the womb of Christ.

The experience impacted me deeply, and I reflected on it continuously. I did have an inkling that it belonged to the realm of the mystical, but I was very reluctant to take my thinking in that direction. Who was I to think I could have had a mystical experience? Instead, I had other angles to consider that related more to the mood of radical detachment that had preceded the whole event.

Alongside my lifelong experiences of becoming detached, as I mentioned earlier, I had also lived my life with a profound feeling of being lost, as if I were dislocated at the very level of my being. From my earliest memories, something about life felt very wrong to me. I felt I was in the wrong place, as if being human caused me to be torn from my true home. And I felt deeply that I did not belong – not just to my family, but also to humanity. I felt that my true home lay somewhere far beyond planet Earth. Of course, as a child I did not have any such fancy language or ideas available to me to describe or understand these feelings; I simply learned to live with a deep and unnameable intuition that I was lost and did not belong.

As a child, I longed to die, so that I could get to where I properly belonged. I took it for granted I would die young once it was realized I was in the wrong place. By *what* or *whom*, I did not know. Not even the image of heaven offered by my Catholic upbringing answered to my intuition about where I truly belonged – probably because in Catholicism there is no guarantee of getting into heaven, whereas I knew there was definitely some place where I would experience perfect belonging.

It was not until I was in my early twenties, when I began to read widely and discovered the angst of 20th-century European existentialists such as Sartre and Camus, that I encountered the language I needed to begin describing these feelings to myself. Their description of unnameable angst and inchoate malaise, and an unfocused anxiety about life in general, resonated deeply with me. But even then, I intuited that the existentialists had gone wrong in concluding that these feelings of angst meant that life was meaningless. I felt that life was incredibly meaningful – I just couldn't figure out what that meaning was. What I intuited, but could not yet articulate, was that our struggle with life points to a spiritual crisis rather than an existential one.

When a mood of detachment came on within me, this sense of being lost and not belonging would intensify greatly. It would also prompt a phenomenal sense of longing and yearning – a desire for something absolutely vast but that I could not name. I longed with my whole being for this thing without ever knowing what I was longing for. It was deeply frustrating to feel an infinite and cosmic desire in me for something bigger than this world, without having the slightest idea of what it could be.

These were difficult feelings to manage as a child, but it never crossed my mind to speak of them to anybody. I sensed it would be dangerous to say anything. No one around me seemed to feel the way I felt. They were all just getting on with life in a way that was difficult for me to do. As I got older, and came to terms with the fact that the early death I had hoped for had not occurred, I was not particularly happy about it. Life just did not match up in any way to my intuition of what it should be like. Not that I could put into words what I thought it should be like – it was more a case of: *I would know it when I saw it, and this definitely was not it!*

There are a few more things about the moods that are worth sharing here because they all became central on my path to discovering that I was becoming a mystic. They come centre stage in Chapter 3, and will also be discussed in Chapter 15, in the guide to awakening. I mentioned earlier that when I was in those 'moods', I used to feel that I was floating between places. As I got older, I began to intuit that this in-between place where I floated was a place of huge significance, because when I was there, the 'atmosphere' seemed to be charged with phenomenal meaning, even though I could not grasp what it was. Often, it would feel as if the air itself were bursting with meaning on a cosmic scale – as if it were holding the very meaning of life – but I had absolutely no idea how to interpret what it might be. It was as if I were being shown something of vast significance but with no instructions on how to understand it; like asking someone with no musical education to write out the musical score of a symphony on a first listen; or like hearing a foreign language and hoping to figure out its meaning just by listening to it – utterly impossible.

The meaning I sensed was indecipherable to me. I did not have the key to unlock or to interpret what I was sensing. I accepted it all as something unusual about myself that I could never speak of to another soul. Looking back, I can say that the atmosphere of the moods was sacred, but at the time I did not recognize it as such. The moods and this 'place' where I floated I now understand as the liminal space where transformation of consciousness occurs. We will look at this, too, in detail in Chapter 15.

> *These moods made me feel deeply connected to what really mattered, even though I did not know what that was.*

It was frustrating to feel myself so close to the highest possible knowing, but unable to grasp it. As the years went by, I realized I preferred to be 'in the mood' and 'close to the answers' even if I could not figure out what they were. I preferred it by far to simply engaging in ordinary life, which I found dull by comparison.

When reflecting on what had happened at Glanleam, I began to realize that the experience of deep peace, and the thought of resting forever in Christ, was the first time I had ever experienced something that could answer to my primordial sense of being lost and not belonging. The sense of homecoming suggested in the idea of becoming one with nature and re-entering the *womb of Christ* gave me my first ever insight into the scale of what was needed to answer my feelings of being lost and not belonging. This was where I would find the meaning I craved. These insights were of course only just beginning to form; they were intuitions without any clear articulation. I was just sensing things at a level below or beyond language.

Seven years would pass before I could make the connection between what happened that night at the edge of the Atlantic and the realization that these moods had always been a precursor to me becoming a mystic.

Even though I was not able to admit to myself at the time that the experience had been a mystical experience, it did prompt me to turn to some of the great Christian mystical writers for guidance, although that guidance proved to be very poor. I started with St John of the Cross, the Spanish mystic from the late medieval period, famous for the eponymous phrase 'dark night of the soul'.

I read two of his books, *Ascent of Mount Carmel* and *Dark Night of the Soul*. Both of these forcefully insisted that if one is receiving unusual spiritual experiences – without being engaged in deep, purposeful and supervised spiritual practices – it must always be assumed that they are coming from the dark side; that we must never consider such experiences to be truly mystical. Instead, we should treat them as a visit from the devil dressed in light. He frightened the life out of me.

He made me think that, in some incomprehensible way, the beautiful experience at Glanleam had been the work of the devil. I was so disheartened. The one avenue of research that I had thought would help me to understand the experience became a dead end. If the experience was not mystical but the work of the devil, I did not want to explore it any further. Even though I had outgrown much of the medieval fearmongering of the Irish Catholicism in which I was raised, the residue of fear it had left within me was still clearly strong enough to ensure that I was not ready to do battle with the devil for my soul.

However, my reading in mysticism ignited a fire in me. I had always been fascinated by the mystics, by their accounts of ecstasy, of leaving their body, losing all sense of identity and joining as one with God, and I admit that I regretted I had not been born a mystic. Now I read their works with much more nuance, hovering somewhere between knowing that something similar had happened to me while also knowing I was not allowed to believe that to be the case.

I became captivated by the topic and voraciously began to read mystical literature and commentary. I read works of mystics such as Catherine of Siena, Julian of Norwich, Rumi and Plotinus. I was spellbound to read of their amazing experiences. I read Rilke, St Francis of Assisi, Plato and St Teresa of Ávila, and they spoke directly to my soul about the one thing that I thought really mattered in life. I felt deeply connected to their stories – they resonated with me, yet I made sure to keep 'a safe distance', given my fear of calling in the devil.

All that I read exhilarated me. I knew I was reading some of the greatest truths of existence, but I also accepted, sadly, that the mystical life was not for me. Their descriptions of union with God, however, and of encountering the real meaning of life, cast a spell on me.

The accounts of their holy experiences gave me a feeling of coming home to what really mattered in life, but I was sufficiently scared by what St John of the Cross had written not to fantasize about trying to make it happen myself. And anyway, the extreme practices of prayer, purgation and asceticism observed by the mystics were far beyond anything I would have considered doing myself. So, while I thought the mystic experience represented the highest imaginable experience of life for the lucky few who attained it, my interest remained resolutely at the level of the intellectual and not the practical. I was not seeking this experience for myself; I did not think I was entitled to it, nor would I have known how to go about making it happen.

The existence of God and a higher realm of goodness was something that was always easy for me to accept. It was not just because it was the teaching of my Christian faith, but also because it seemed manifestly obvious to me that these ideas were true. As a child, I felt myself loved by Jesus, by God and by my guardian angel. As an adult, the sheer beauty and brilliance of creation testified to an intelligent design by an infinite and beautiful mind. I always found it easy to identify with my spiritual side, knowing intuitively that there was more going on than that which we could see in front of us. I was comfortable with the spiritual, and also comforted by the concept of heaven and a higher form of existence, knowing that at some point we would get away from this world of pain and go to a place of deep peace and endless love. I knew instinctively that our spiritual self would outlive our physical bodies. I did not need any faith to teach me this. However, I was not a spiritual seeker in any way. I had no religious or spiritual calling.

It had been very important to me, in my early adulthood, to reject the superstitious component of my childhood religion: *if you do not do x, you will go to hell.* I simply knew that God did not work that way. I practised my religion in my own way and refused to feel the guilt I was told I ought to feel. And now I equally reject the superstitious component of some alternative spiritual practices.

My spirituality was something that I took for granted, like a nice reassuring hum in the background of my life. I did not pay much attention to it but trusted it would be there if or when I needed it, much like the emergency services. I lived a very full life and had as many moral failings as the next person, probably more. I suppose I lived my life on twin tracks, on the one hand possessed of a strong love for God, but on the other very much enjoying a life of partying, drinking and carousing. I did not particularly care about the contradiction.

But I did think that it must be sublime to have immediate contact with God. I was in awe at the idea of leaving one's body and entering a state of ecstasy, of losing one's identity and merging with God. I thought it must be the greatest imaginable experience, but it did not cross my mind that it might become a possibility for me. I read about mysticism as one might read about the Apollo mission to outer space – something that 'other people' did.

As the years went by, I all but forgot the experience at Glanleam. The possibility that I could become a mystic never entered my mind. It never arose even as an idle thought. In fact, I specifically guarded against such thoughts entering my mind after what I had read in St John of the Cross.

⁓

CHAPTER 2

AN EXPLOSION
IN MY MIND

*'At the depth of the psyche
is sacred ground.'*
CLARISSA PINKOLA ESTÉS

A ll that I have shared so far was going on in the background of my life and in the privacy of my mind. In my regular day-to-day reality, I was busy living my very full and ordinary life, and lots was happening there, too. There had been highs and lows over the years, but one major life challenge that I had faced was suffering with undiagnosed postnatal depression for well over a year after my first child was born.

Looking back, I can see that this was the singular event that redirected the course of my life. It was the archetypal breakdown event, or the break with the old, that each of us must experience, in one form or another, if we are to come into our maturity and authenticity.

I was 33 years old, the very time that life invites us to move beyond our youthful, egoic and self-focused way of being in the world. Some lucky people manage this transition with grace and ease, but others of us do not actually hear the call to maturity. In such cases, life itself will contribute a crisis to let us know we are off track in some fundamental way. When this happens, we collapse in a heap, fall apart and have to build ourselves back up, cell by cell, bone by bone and sometimes even breath by breath, but this time, into a truer, more authentic version of who we really are.

The crisis that life gave me was postnatal depression, delivered with the force of an explosion in my mind. I did not know it at the time, but this was the first step towards becoming my true self. In the language of the heroine's journey – it was the first stage of hearing the 'call'.

In traditional cultures, all major life transitions were marked by initiation rituals and ceremonies in the community that truly supported and guided the individual to engage with the deep psychic energies associated with important life changes. The person was supported to engage consciously, psychologically, energetically and spirituality with the shift into a more mature level of consciousness.

In the West, we no longer pay attention to the psychological or spiritual component of the transition into a new stage of life. Instead, we have graduation ceremonies and birthday parties for which we buy a new dress and probably get drunk – entirely missing the psychological and spiritual element of the life transition. By 33, I had bought lots of new dresses and drunk many bottles of champagne, without ever discovering who I really was.

When my precious daughter Laragh was born in 2001, unknown to me, several psychic and energetic currents met like live wires in my mind, sending shock waves through my psyche. This psychic maelstrom manifested as postnatal depression and it did for me what every good 'breakdown' is meant to do – it unilaterally dismantled the structures of my ego and the identity that I had outgrown but which I had not yet let go. It collapsed the structure of my ego, and it revealed deeper truths to me about myself and my life that I needed to explore. Life could not go on in the same old way. It was time for radical change. It was time to grow up.

The reason I am sharing this very personal story here is to acknowledge that there are very real struggles on the road to awakening. It takes hard work to come into our truth and breakdown events, life crises and suffering seem to be unavoidable parts of real growth. My guess is that many of you reading this book will have faced, or are facing, your own version of crisis or breakdown, and I want to reach out to you with empathy and encourage you to know the deep purpose that our struggles serve on our path to authenticity. When we let life to do its thing in us, we will be redesigned for the better.

These crises undoubtedly look like disasters at the time, but in retrospect they prove – or will prove – to be the making of us.

They also frequently start us out on a whole new path in life. Nonetheless, while we are in the middle of the crisis, we resist it with all of our might. In my case, at that time, what I was resisting was growing up and becoming mature. Yet, what I now know for sure is that there cannot be an awakening until we have faced this inner work of becoming mature and authentic. Psychological maturity is an essential milestone on the path and, in fact, it brings us to the door of our awakening.

> *We always come out on the far side of these life events stronger, more authentic, more confident and more courageous.*

Of course, I knew none of these deep and wise truths as I happily and naively embraced the experience of becoming a mother. And I may as well admit here that naivety and optimism have been hallmarks of my personality all of my life. I walk into situations with wide-eyed wonder, curiosity and enthusiasm (if not innocence), often missing the warning signs that keep other people out. I also have a dogged determination to follow through on anything I undertake, so when others might see that they have bitten off more than they can chew, I keep chewing. I have become grateful for these character traits, however, because that eager curiosity provides me with big life learnings that otherwise I may well have missed. The doggedness ultimately gets me out on the far side and the optimism keeps a smile on my face. So, whereas some people just have skin in the game of life, I have thrown my whole self in.

When my daughter was born, I expected to be overjoyed. My pregnancy had been very happy and I was looking forward to becoming a mother with every ounce of my being. But being pregnant and giving birth are two very different things, and as I went into labour I was overwhelmed by the enormity of the experience. I almost physically felt something explode and shatter inside me, and I seemed to see pieces of myself fly like shards of glass out of the hospital windows in every direction across the city. It would take me a long time to gather up those pieces of myself and put them back together again into a stronger, truer and more robust version of who I am. Yet, during the five days I spent in the maternity hospital, no one on the entire medical team picked up on what had happened to me. And, being the perfectionist that I was, I could not admit to anyone that something might have gone wrong.

Postnatal depression was not on my radar. I had happily skipped over those chapters in my pregnancy books, so I was totally unaware that some of the feelings I was experiencing were definite indicators of the condition. From all that I have since learned about postnatal depression, it is clear to me now that, even before I left the hospital with my new baby, I was showing definite signs – if not full-blown symptoms – of postnatal depression. Nevertheless, I was sent home, and I just had to presume that the confused, overwhelming mixture of joy and fear I was experiencing was perfectly normal for a new mother.

It was impossible to admit, even to myself, that things were not turning out as I had expected. A gulf opened up between how I was feeling and how I wanted to be feeling. Unable to admit this to myself or anyone else, I fluctuated between being happy, coping and sometimes enjoying life as a new mother, but at other times being overwhelmed, crying a lot and feeling despair but not knowing why.

Because I did not understand that something was actually wrong with me, I pushed myself, harder than was humane, to keep going and to find a way to be happy. With no insight into what was wrong, I could only conclude that this was the way it was meant to be, and that it was true – motherhood really was hard.

During those months, I described to my doctor much of what I was experiencing – things that I now know are classic symptoms of postnatal depression – but she glossed over them and sent me home with absolutely no insight into what was wrong. There was a major disconnect between what was happening in my life and what I wanted to be happening, but I could not admit the chasm to myself.

With no words to name what was wrong, I lived in a desperate in-between state – feeling compelled to present to the world as if everything was fine, because I had no way of explaining why it was *not* fine. I did not feel entitled to complain when I had a beautiful, healthy baby and there was no reason to think I was suffering at a different level to anyone else I knew who had had a baby at the same time.

At the deepest level of my psyche, I had needed my experience of becoming a mother to be very successful. I had some vaguely conscious notion that by becoming a 'perfect mother' to my daughter I would heal whatever scars I carried. My mother's mother had died during the time my mother was pregnant with me. I discovered this when I visited my grandmother's grave, where I read '1968' – the year of her death and my birth – etched in stone under her name. A shock ran through me that made me feel as if I, too, had been turned to stone. I felt the impact of the shock physically in my body, and in a split second I knew this was information I had been missing all of my life. My mother's grief and mourning at losing her mother had undoubtedly made her experience of being pregnant with me difficult for her. I have no doubt that I picked up my mother's sadness during my time in her womb.

This coping/not-coping rollercoaster lasted for 18 months, right up until I was about 10 weeks pregnant with our second child. And then, one afternoon, sitting in my kitchen, crying, I heard my inner voice saying: *I have postnatal depression.* It was inspired and I later came to recognize it as a gift from my son, then growing in my womb. But in that moment every fragile coping mechanism in my mind came crashing down. There was no need to pretend anymore. The devastation of failing at the most important undertaking of my life was indescribable. There was no suggestion of turning towards myself with love or compassion – there was only pain, self-judgement and an overwhelming sense that I had failed my daughter.

Climbing the stone stairs to my first appointment with Professor Anthony McCarthy, a specialist in postnatal depression, represented an outsized failure in a world that demanded perfection. I cried my way through that first appointment, sobbing my sorry tale to him. When I finally paused, he said to me, with a gentle kindness that I will never forget, 'You needed acknowledgement.' His words felt like a balm to my broken soul. They landed as a profound truth. On so many different levels I needed acknowledgement – we all do – and him articulating that became a foundational acknowledgement in my life.

Thus began the long road to healing. My postnatal depression became the archetypal breakdown-to-breakthrough. Little did I know then that it would become the inner journey through the psychic forest, the dark night of the soul that would finally introduce me to my true and authentic self, and would culminate 14 years later in pure mystical experiences. Clarissa Pinkola Estés, author of the brilliant *Women Who Run With the Wolves*, wrote that at the depths of the psyche lies sacred ground. And this is where our inner work brings all of us – to sacred ground and to the door of our awakening.

After my son, Cuan, was born, I gave up work as a barrister. I knew I needed to take better care of myself, and a big part of that was being at home with my children and learning how to be a 'good enough mother' instead of the perfect mother I had been trying to be. It was a beautiful time and I enjoyed being a new mother again, experiencing it as challenging and rewarding in equal measure, but no longer overwhelming.

One incredible upside of this major psychic awakening was that the floodgates of my creativity opened and I turned to journalling as a way to process what was going on for me. It was wonderfully cathartic to write about all that I was living through, and there was healing in getting things down onto the page. I wrote stories for my children; a memoir about my postnatal depression; short stories; poetry and articles for the magazine *The Gloss*. What initially functioned as a release valve soon became an enjoyable hobby, then a passion and now a career.

Creative writing began to flow out of me like a river through an unstopped dam.

When the time came for me think about going back to work, I could not contemplate returning to the legal world. Everything about it jarred with my soul. The thought of courtrooms, litigation, judges, cross-examination, law books, legal pleadings, research, tension, aggression, egos and pressure – they all clashed violently with how I knew I wanted to be: calm, peaceful, authentic and creative. My greatest desire was to become a writer, so I decided that instead of returning to my law practice I would begin all over again and go back to university to study English and philosophy. This was not a straightforward decision in terms of our family finances, but I was prepared to sacrifice much in order to be true to who I was becoming.

Studying was a great joy and I felt deeply fulfilled in my life. The whirl of dinner parties and nights out was over. I was happier than I had ever been and I felt that I had found my soul's true calling. In my final year, I was accepted into the MA in creative writing for the following academic year. I felt that everything in my life had finally fallen into place and my career as a writer was taking shape. As I was soon to find out, however, God had entirely different plans for me and for my life.

In retrospect, I can see that there was a clear intelligence to the path of my life right from the very beginning. Now that I understand that life itself is pure intelligence, it is obvious that all of our lives are following an intelligent trajectory to bring us into our greatest and best self – *if* we cooperate, *if* we read the signs, *if* we decipher the meaning of things, *if* we trust, *if* we go with the breakdowns, *if* we do our soul work, *if* we develop acceptance, *if* we learn to truly love ourselves and others, and *if* we entrust ourselves over to a higher power.

And all those *ifs* are natural milestones of psychological and spiritual growth.

Now I can see how all the pain and the deep learning experiences of my life were connected, related and consciously leading me somewhere. At first, I thought it was leading me to understand my own life, but just as that insight was forming, just as I was beginning to understand how my life hung together, I suddenly broke through to a profound spiritual awakening. Now I realize that spiritual awakening is a gift that is offered to anyone who will make the effort to understand the meaning of life. Now I know that spiritual awakening lies on the other side of pain, on the other side of growth, on the other side of healing, on the other side of authenticity, on the other side of self-acceptance and on the other side of self-love.

~

CHAPTER 3

A MIND ON FIRE

From 'I think, therefore I am' to 'I am, therefore I love.'

Even though I had learned so much about authenticity through the experience of becoming a mother, I still had much to learn about the essential connectedness of humanity. When I began to study philosophy, I still lived with the Western mindset of disconnect: a mindset that assumed there was little old me, or you, all on our own, making our small efforts to get by in life. And then there was a great big world out there, separate to us, largely alien to us, with its own hidden meaning that was minimally comprehensible, even to the greatest minds. I had no feeling that any of our lives really mattered in the overall scheme of things; or that we belonged in any meaningful way to a greater 'whole'. I considered that the presence of each of us here was just the wildly random chance of our birth – nothing more.

I was studying philosophy because I was interested in the meaning of life, but I did not think there was any meaning attached to my own life, or to anyone else's life. I just thought that we were caught up in a big experience of creation that probably did not even know we were here.

The 17th-century French philosopher René Descartes is usually blamed for this Western mindset of disconnect. His famous intuition, 'I think, therefore I am,' is seen as the line in the sand after which humanity lost its sense of connection with the whole by privileging private thinking – his 'I think' – above interrelatedness with others and the world. Yet, I do not think that Descartes was saying anything new; rather, he was reflecting back to us our fundamental attitude towards life. Maybe by naming it he unleashed its power to take over entirely and gave us permission to live lives of radical disconnection, separation and division. But given all that I have learned and experienced since then, with all of my heart I want to rewrite Descartes' famous idiom and change it from 'I think, therefore I am' to 'I am, therefore I love.'

Studying philosophy did for me what four decades of religious practice had been unable to do. It overturned my sense of disconnect and isolation, and it opened the eyes of my mind to such an extent that it brought me to the very door of my mystical awakening. It gave me a whole new understanding of God, of life, of myself, of our essential connection to each other and of the inherent divinity of existence. Philosophy set my mind on fire in a way that my religion had never been able to do.

One evening, during the second year of my BA, I was sitting at my kitchen table preparing for a tutorial on the philosopher

F.W.J. Schelling when I read the most beautiful and radical idea I had ever heard expressed: that nature is God giving birth to itself. I did not just read this sentence – I experienced it as forcefield of truth that penetrated my being. The magnitude of the idea entered my soul and seared into the deepest part of me, making me feel as if I had been waiting my whole life to hear this truth. Such an exquisite rendering of the intimate connection between that which creates and that which is created left me awed. The idea felt sacred.

Something shifted in me that night. Although I had no words to describe what had happened, Schelling's beautiful idea subtly became the frame through which I have looked at life ever since: that God, in birthing its own self as beautiful nature, also gives birth to us as parts of nature, and as parts of God. Maybe, after all, I did belong to something bigger than myself; maybe God did know I was here; maybe I was important; maybe we are all important. These were new ideas that I now carried with reverence in my heart.

At the start of my final year, in September 2014, my precious father passed away, leaving me heartbroken. As I stood in that liminal space between life and death, grieving for my dad, and contemplating deeply the meaning of life, we began studying the work of the philosopher Martin Heidegger. When I read his description of a certain 'mood of anxiety that temporarily moves people out of ordinary consciousness', my whole being reacted viscerally. He was describing, exactly, my own strange moods. He spoke of a mood that sometimes comes over people and moves them out of ordinary consciousness into a detached space where things no longer make sense, and where one feels strangely removed from everyday concerns. It was as uncanny as it was amazing to discover at last someone who shared and understood my secret experience of these moods. I was riveted by all that I read, in the same way that I had been riveted by Schelling's wonderful metaphor of birth.

But Heidegger wrote about this mood as if it were happening to everybody all of the time, so why, then, do we never hear anything about it? In 46 years, that was my first encounter with someone who understood these moods. Maybe many of you reading this book also experience these moods that I have been describing, and will have experienced this 'floating' to another level of consciousness and becoming detached from ordinary reality. And maybe, like me, you have never appreciated that these moods actually have major significance. And maybe, like me, you have wondered whether you were just a little bit crazy.

Heidegger also wrote that these moods correspond to a 'call of conscience' or a 'call to authenticity', so that when the mood comes over us, we are entering our authenticity in such a way that we come into contact with our truest self and with 'primordial Being'. This gave him his famous phrase, 'Become who you already are.' He wrote that, when the mood passes, we return in our mind to the everyday world and go about our business, but now with an increased desire to strive for authenticity. What Heidegger called 'primordial Being', a religious or spiritual person would call God.

If you share this experience of these moods, and if this the first time you have come upon an explanation for our unusual way of being in the world, then I share your relief, and sense of awe, at finally discovering that these difficult-to-understand moods are in fact crucial experiences on the path to our authenticity and on our path to awakening.

> *It was deeply emotional for me to discover, at last, something meaningful about my secret moods and my strange way of being in the world.*

I was touched, heartened, encouraged and joyous finally to have some insight into what my moods and feelings meant. It felt like a parting gift from my precious dad. At last I was not alone – I was not crazy. I was very excited.

All this resonated in me as truth and gave me a new understanding of my secret self. This insight became a guiding light in my life, and turned out to be the key that, just a few weeks later, opened up a wild new world of riches for me. But before I share that incredible experience with you, I need to mention one more important idea about longing; an idea that resonates with so many people who are on the brink of awakening and will probably resonate with many of you reading this book. It proved to be a crucial insight for me, and maybe it will for you, too.

It comes from the philosopher Emmanuel Levinas, who blew me clean away with his description of a 'deep and vast, impossible to satisfy desire' that we feel when we discover the impossibility of fully knowing an 'other' [person], or knowing the great other of God. He called it 'metaphysical desire', and wrote that by its nature it is 'impossible to satisfy'. The philosophical shocks were coming hard and fast for me – he was describing exactly my lifelong experience of *deep and frustrating, cosmic-sized longing* for something vast and unnameable that had always been impossible to satisfy. I was transfixed and dumbstruck. My longing was, at last, meaningful. Even though I did not yet appreciate that the focus of my longing was God, at least it now had a name. My sense of relief was huge. Once more, I was comforted that maybe I was not crazy.

All this learning about my moods and metaphysical desire was not just in my head, it was also in my body. These insights felt like a profound homecoming. For 46 years, I had lived with these moods and this longing, and now, in one semester, during the greatest grief of my life, I had found the answers I needed. This all touched me deeply in the place in my soul where my fascination with mysticism lived. There was something much bigger going on in my inner life than I could ever have imagined. Now I had intimations that my life experiences transcended the ordinary finite world in a very significant way. It did not cross my mind that there was still more to be discovered about all this. It was enough to know these things were meaningful, and that alone would have been sufficient for me to have died happy. But there was indeed more to come.

When the mood of detachment next came over me just a few weeks later, on 19 December 2014, I was by then almost excited to experience it for the first time ever with a modicum of insight and understanding. It was a Friday afternoon, my college exams were over, my kids were at friends' houses and my husband was not expected home until evening. I had no commitments and was free to do as I wished. So, with a great sense of surrender, as the mood developed, I fully and freely offered myself up to the feeling of becoming detached. I just surrendered, come what may. I welcomed it, curious to engage meaningfully with it at last – after all, 46 years is a long time not to understand something. I went for a walk by the river that runs through our local park and, as I walked, the wildest experience of my life began to unfold inside me. I became both witness and participant to an epic event taking place inside my own being.

Powerful energy began building in my body, filling every part of me. It was expanding and pulsating inside me with urgency, filling me to bursting, making me feel as if it wanted to rip me open at the seams so that it could escape out of me and into the world. It was fierce and urgent, like the rumbling of a volcano about to erupt. I felt as if I had the wild power of Mother Nature inside me, as if there were a hurricane raging in me. I felt as if I could explode from the power of it, but I was not scared – I was fascinated. There was something inside me that wanted to burst out of me, but I had no idea what it was or how to get it out. I sensed something wanting to be born out of me, but I had no idea how to birth it. Then I had an urgent realization that the reason it could not get out was because it was blocked, and I was the block. I realized, *I am what is stopping this energy from coming out of me.* But I did not know what to do. It crossed my mind that if I had been born a whirling dervish I could have begun to dance, and I would have danced it into wild expression with my body.

Then somehow, I understood that whatever it was that wanted to come out, wanted to come out in words. It wanted me to speak, or to deliver a message for it, but I had no idea what it wanted me to say. I had no idea what words I could use to express this powerful but incoherent message that I felt exploding inside me. It was a message without content. There was something completely unknown in me, wildly urging me to speak, without telling me what to say. I had no idea how to let this powerful energy express itself through me. My frustration was intense.

As I continued walking, I gave my whole being over to this incredible experience. I was not at all frightened. Levinas and Heidegger had given me a context for at least a tentative understanding, so I did not try to stop it – I gave it free rein.

I walked for over an hour, and when I came home from the park, the wild and epic experience continued inside me throughout the evening. As soon as I could, I went to my study and began to write in my journal, trying to capture something of it as it happened, even though it was beyond my understanding.

Then the energy changed from a desire to be expressed – maybe because I was now writing – and began to express itself as pure desire or longing. Pure longing was expressing itself inside me, on the same scale as the energy that I had felt trying to burst out of me in the park – a hurricane or a volcano about to erupt inside me. But this energy of longing was *not* trying to get out of me. It seemed to be just showing itself to me, revealing itself to me, not asking anything of me. Then I understood that it was showing itself to me specifically so that I would *know* it.

It was decidedly not *my* longing. Rather, I was feeling pure longing itself manifesting in me somehow. And even more than that, this pure longing did not want anything. It was explicitly showing me that it did not want to be satisfied, that it did not *need* to be satisfied – that, in fact, it would be impossible to satisfy it!

All I could do was to let the experience happen in me. Longing was showing me that its nature, and its way of being, was simply *to long*. In being true to its nature, it must remain an unsatisfied desire. This was a paradox of seismic proportions – a longing that did not seek satisfaction was alien to me. Yet, it was showing me that all it wanted to do was to long; that there was nothing in the entire known world or universe that was great enough to satisfy this longing that I was feeling inside me. Nothing could satisfy it; nothing could stop this longing. It would continue forever. That is the scale of the power I was feeling in me. It was drawing me into a swirling eddy of pure desire that did not want anything.

I felt that the entire world could offer itself in sacrifice to this longing, but it would be dismissed as a mere crumb.

Then I intuited that to satisfy this longing would destroy its nature, and that *that* would be a creation-altering tragedy. This was a 'thing' or an experience (it is difficult to find the right word), of beauty, power and majesty. It would be sacrilege to interfere with its nature. I realized that longing was sharing itself with me, revealing itself to me, offering itself to me as a gift, for the sole purpose of helping me to know it. It seemed to me that I was being taught the lesson that, when it comes to cosmic desire, we ought to accept the paradox that a desire left unsatisfied is, in fact, satisfied. That its nature is to remain unsatisfied.

As I completed my lengthy journalling, I found myself inspired to write that the whole event related to a pain in my womb, or in my mother's womb, or in some other womb. It was unclear whose womb. I have no idea how I came to form those thoughts about a womb pain.

Eight days later, on Christmas Day, I received the message that I should go to Séan Boylan's herbal clinic.

CHAPTER 4

MEETING MY SPIRITUAL MASTER

'Be at peace, as I AM Peace.'
VOICE OF GOD

As I wrote earlier, what little I understood of the message about Séan Boylan's clinic being a place I needed to go to, I had related to the fact that two years previously I had gone partially deaf in my left ear. It had been investigated by modern medicine and no one could explain how it had happened, but all agreed it was irreversible. They could offer nothing beyond a hearing aid, which I declined because I intended to regain my hearing.

As a result, I had started to explore some complementary health modalities, including kinesiology and amatsu. This was a new departure for me in life. My father was a consultant medical doctor with a very Western scientific approach towards health, and this was the environment in which I had grown up. I knew almost nothing about alternative healthcare or energy work, but

I was open and curious about anything that could help to restore my hearing. It was in this context that I understood the message I had received: *That's the place for me!* I presumed that it related somehow to getting help for my deafness.

When Séan's clinic reopened after the Christmas holidays, I rang and asked for an appointment with anyone who was available. The first therapist I attended said she could not help and suggested an appointment with a colleague who she thought might be able to help. And so it was that I was introduced to the brilliant craniosacral therapist, David, who has been helping me ever since. Being treated by David feels like handing oneself over to a master practitioner whose skill at reading and supporting the person, on all three levels of the physical, psychological and spiritual, is nothing short of remarkable. The most significant aspect of craniosacral therapy is the process of somato-emotional release, which is designed to help release trauma stored in the tissues of the body.

To meet David is to know you have met someone very special. He has a quiet, understated yet commanding presence. There is a deep wisdom within him and he quickly inspired complete confidence in me. As he worked, it was obvious that he knew what he was doing at a deeper level than I had ever encountered before. His work feels almost holy – so deep is his reverence for what he is doing and for the person who he is helping. I had never met anyone like him before. I believed that, with him, I would recover my hearing. I presumed it would be my physical hearing, but it turned out to be my spiritual hearing. David's quiet, modest but critical role in opening me to fully receive and understand the gift of becoming a mystic tells me that the voice in my head on that Christmas Day was guiding me directly to him.

At that first appointment with David, he helped me to realize that I still had very deep unexpressed grief at losing my father. I cried a lot. At the end of the session, David said to me, 'Your body is crying out for you to meditate.' And that simple observation changed the course of my life.

I left the clinic feeling as though something profound had happened to me by meeting David, but without knowing what that 'something' was. As I walked to my car I asked myself, *What just happened?* But I had no answer. It was about two years later, when reading about *The Tibetan Book of the Dead*, that I learned of the Buddhist idea of transmission of an awakened mind. Buddhism believes that we each have a spiritual master and, when we are ready, we will meet them and they will catalyse our spiritual awakening by transmitting their awakened mind to us. Given what has unfolded for me while in his care, I knew that this idea described exactly what happened to me when I met David. My nascent awakening was catalysed: his awakened mind awakened mine. Somehow, he had been destined to be the guardian of my spiritual awakening but – as is always the story of my life – I did not understand it at the time.

As I drove home after the first session with David, a beautiful song I had never heard before began playing on the car radio and it immediately touched me in a profoundly meaningful way, although I did not know why that should be so. It was called *This Is the Day the Lord Hath Made*, an anthem composed by John Rutter for the British royal wedding of Prince William and his bride, Kate. It was sung by the choir of Westminster Abbey and recorded live at their wedding in 2011.

It was very beautiful and, as I listened, the words seared into the depths of my heart. They seemed to be speaking directly to me, as if they were delivering a personal message, yet on the face of it, they had no apparent application to me or to my life. Even though I could not understand why, I felt deeply that I had been intended to hear this exact song, at this exact time. The music was exquisite. Here are some of the lyrics:

> *This is the day... which the Lord hath made*
>   *We will rejoice and be glad in it. [...]*
> *For he shall give his angels charge over thee: to keep thee in all*
>   *thy ways. [...]*
> *The Lord himself is thy keeper: the Lord is thy defence upon thy*
>   *right hand; [...]*
> *The Lord shall preserve thee from all evil: [...]*
> *The Lord shall preserve thy going out and thy coming in: [...]*
> *From this time forth for evermore. [...]*
> *He shall defend thee under his wings.*
> *Be strong, and he shall comfort thine heart, [...]*
> *And put thou thy trust... in the Lord.*
> *Put thou thy trust in the Lord*

It gave me serious goose bumps – but why would God be telling me that today was a special day? Why would God now be giving angels charge over me? Why should I need God as my keeper and protector from now on? In what way would my going out and my coming in be in need of heavenly protection? Why did I need to be courageous? Why did I now doubly need to put my trust in God? I had no idea, but I felt very charged by the messages I believed I was receiving through the song. I discovered later that the lyrics are all drawn from the Psalms of Moses and King David, and this has given me a much clearer understanding of why the hymn impacted me as deeply as it did that day.

When I arrived home, I parked my car, and as I walked towards the house, something prompted me to look up at the wall above the front door. And there, on this cold January day, in the middle of winter, among the bare branches of our climbing rose bush, two red roses were in full bloom side by side on a single branch. A thrill ran through me. I knew instinctively that they were a sign from my beloved father that he had been a part of all that had transpired that morning. By leaning out of my bedroom window I was able to cut the roses and bring them into the house. I still have them, dried, in a vase on the mantlepiece in my study.

After lunch I decided to try my hand at meditating straight away. I had no experience of meditation. It was not part of the culture in which I had grown up, and tragically, meditation does not form part of Christian religious formation. I had never given any thought to meditation – anything that I knew about it I had picked up along the way, and it was not much. The only assumption I may have had was that it was a calming technique.

I presumed the reason David had recommended it to me was to help with my grief over losing my dad.

Following my instincts, I lit a candle and placed a photo of Dad on the kitchen table. I put the roses in a glass of water beside his photo, and chose a CD of Gregorian chant. As soon as I sat down at the table, a flood of tears came out of me. I cried for about two hours. So much grief had been pent up inside me. I loved my father with all of my heart.

From that day on I began to 'meditate' daily. I had no real idea of what I was meant to do, so I just sat quietly and let it unfold. I had no idea if I was doing it correctly or incorrectly, but I liked it. I did not even know if there was a right or a wrong way to meditate. I had a completely open mind, with no preconceptions about what might be involved. All I knew was that meditators sat very still, so that is what I tried to do.

I knew nothing about the breath or mantras. It was with complete innocence that I approached it. And sometimes I wonder whether it was my naivety that enabled so much to happen so quickly. I am sure it was the first time in my life that I had done something with absolutely no preconceptions or expectations about it, with no idea of how it ought to be done, or what ought to happen. I approached it completely free of context or purpose. I guess it would have satisfied my beloved Meister Eckhart's advice to 'live without a why'.

Maybe the innocence of my approach was the thing that opened it up for me, because it turns out that I was a natural at meditation. It was easy for me to sit without fidgeting, to still my mind and to enter deep silence. Sitting for 20 minutes without being much distracted came easily to me. Maybe my lifelong experience of moods of detachment had prepared me for this. I felt great peace when I sat to meditate. Nothing tangible happened at first. I did not expect anything to happen – I did not know things *could* happen. I just enjoyed the experience of sitting still. As a matter of course, however, I found that in the stillness I reached out in my mind for the divine, especially Jesus and Mary Magdalene, my favourites. It seemed to me the most natural thing to do.

In retrospect, I can see that I did have the unconscious assumption that becoming still opened a space for God, but I could not have articulated that to myself at the time. It was just instinctive. So, yes, on reflection, I had an intuition that meditation was an opportunity to commune with God in some way, but the way I had it was that meditation was the art of stillness and – *as a side effect* – you got to talk to God. I did not realize that communing with God was the whole point of the exercise! My naivety makes me laugh now.

A favourite line of mine from the Bible has always been, 'Be still and know that I am God.' I was intrigued by what such stillness might be like. I often repeated these words at the start of my meditation, and soon enough, strange and beautiful things began to occur during meditation that dramatically altered the course of my life.

The mood that I wrote about in the last chapter – the one that had come over me in December, had taken over my whole being as if I had a hurricane raging inside me, had asked me to give a message without telling me what to say, and had morphed into impossible-to-satisfy longing – did not lift in the usual way. Instead, it held me somehow estranged from the world and gave me a heightened sense of awareness that made me alert with an uncanny sense of intuition, but not about anything in particular. It did not bother me. I liked it. I was in mourning for my father, and it also seemed a good state for someone immersed in philosophical studies and writing a novel.

It suited me to be in this mood and to be living somewhat at a remove from ordinary life.

Only when I was re-reading my journals to put my story together in preparation for writing this book did I notice that this mood used to 'peak' on the day of an appointment with David. Unusual things would happen, but I did not connect one with the other for a long time.

My fourth appointment with David was scheduled for an afternoon in late March 2015. During the morning hours of that day, my detached mood intensified dramatically in a way that had never happened before. I became agitated and had very heightened awareness, but not of anything in particular. I had a strong sense of premonition, that something *big* was imminent, but I had no idea what it was. My feeling of detachment became pronounced, the *metaphysical desire* was intense, the frustration deeply uncomfortable. I felt decidedly ill at ease, and I was glad I had the session with David booked for later that day. I did not think what was happening was related to the appointment, but I thought David would help in some way. Not, of course, that I was going to tell him a word about how I was feeling – I still thought I was attending him for deafness in my left ear. These secret experiences were still deeply private. I would not have known where to begin to try to explain them to anyone else. It was as much as I could do to try to make sense of it for myself, and I was making no sense of it at all that day.

But as David worked on me that afternoon, I felt myself falling into an unearthly state of peace and I felt as if I were crossing or floating over to somewhere incredibly peaceful. When I got there, I experienced myself to be gently placing my infant daughter back into my womb, as a place of safety and peace for her, and for me, too. The whole thing was unbelievable. I felt the most sublime feeling of stillness and wellbeing. I felt as if I had fallen so deeply into myself that I might never get back out again, and it was beautiful.

I was so deep in this state of peace that when the session ended, I could not and did not return to ordinary consciousness. I found it difficult to get my body up off the table – it felt like a dead weight. I struggled to engage with David's chat as I paid and said goodbye. I could not get back from that place I had gone to. It did not cross my mind to say anything to David about it. How could

I tell him I had gone somewhere and had not come back when I was standing right there in front of him? Anyway, I would not have known how to put into words what I was feeling.

For the whole journey home, a vibrant rainbow arched perfectly across the sky in front of me from east to west. I had never experienced a rainbow like it in my life. It had a powerful and vibrant presence in the sky. Its colours were intense. It was huge and seemed to be there for a purpose – somehow it seemed to be there for me, to protect me. I read it as a phenomenal sign of divine affirmation that whatever had happened during the session was blessed. It seemed miraculous that the rainbow could remain stable there for the whole length of my journey home – over 40 minutes. Even when I turned off the motorway for the last part of the journey, the rainbow remained directly in front of me until I reached my house.

It was not until I was writing this book and putting all the pieces of my story together that I saw the remarkable symmetry and connection between this experience with David and the Glanleam experience of being brought into sublime peace, seven years earlier. It is only now, and admittedly with a great sense of wonder, that I am connecting the dots between my different life experiences. Only now can I discern the path and see how each stage of my awakening was plotted with significant stepping stones that, unbeknown to me, were intelligently marking the path on my life's journey to mystical awakening.

In the days and weeks following that experience with David, I did not fully come back from wherever I had gone. I reflected intensely on what had happened, intuiting that it was connected to my moods and my *metaphysical desire*, but I could not figure out in what way they were connected. My mind was busy trying to piece everything together like a jigsaw, but I struggled to make sense of it.

Soon enough, however, I began to notice a feeling of satisfaction in me that was not mine; rather, it was the mood itself expressing, in *me*, its *own* satisfaction. It was indicating that *it* had 'succeeded'; suggesting that *it* had at last achieved whatever it was it had longed for in me, all of my life. It was as if this mood within me had a mind or a consciousness of its own and was expressing its *own* sense of satisfaction with whatever it had achieved, in me, on David's table.

The oddness of this is hard to convey – to have another mind or consciousness inside my own, yet without my being stark raving mad. At the physical level, it would be as strange as hearing your eye saying it was pleased with its blink; or your lungs expressing pleasure at having just drawn a breath; or your hand congratulating itself for how it had just picked up that pen.

At the time, I was only able to articulate all this to myself in a very rudimentary way, but I knew for sure that the mood *itself* was pleased with what it had achieved. I did not notice the similarity between this consciousness of the mood and the December experience of feeling the consciousness of longing within me. The latter had been a powerful, consuming and intense experience, whereas this was much more ordinary by comparison, although not one bit ordinary at all.

I myself had no sense of achievement: I was feeling its sense of achievement without knowing what had actually been achieved.

I had absolutely no proof or explanation for these outlandish thoughts, but I had them nonetheless. I had a profound sense that the mood was pleased that a milestone had been reached. I did not give any thought to what that milestone was or what the implications for me might be. I still did not understand that my whole life was deeply in play in the operation of these strange events. And it is only now, in writing this paragraph, that I am realizing that the experience with David had brought me into the higher realm; the realm of deep peace, of higher consciousness; in other words – the *mystical* realm. Now I realize that I was witnessing, watching, experiencing or living through a milestone of my consciousness expanding and being transformed.

In the same month that these things were happening, something else very strange caught my attention on another rose bush in my garden. On a white rose bush at the centre of a bed of roses, on one thin branch, three of the five leaves were pure white and the other two were exactly half green and half white. I was mystified. It deeply felt like a sign and I wondered what it might mean.

Fascinated, I began to observe and follow the development of those leaves – even more so when a tiny rose, far smaller than all the others on the bush, began to grow on that same thin branch. As the summer months wore on, more and more sprays of pure white leaves grew on this specific branch but on no other branch of the entire rose bush. I began to take photographs to record and document what I absolutely regarded as a miracle. Each new spray of leaves on this particular branch would begin growing as a vibrant shade of red, but as they grew bigger, the red would fade to pure, almost luminous white – like a living version of the Christ bottle in Aura-Soma.

When that first tiny rose began to form, its outer protective petals were also pure white. It had absolutely no green on it at all, and its stem was pink. It was the only rose to grow on that particular branch that year, although there were tens of other white roses growing normally on other branches of the bush. I watched over the growth of this little rose like a mother watching her newborn, with complete fascination and awe. It was very slow to bloom, taking months to grow and begin to open. The day it finally did burst open into its exquisite wholeness was the day my mother died.

I had a deep intuition that this was all a sign of the presence of Mary Magdalene. I knew by now that the white rose is said to be her special symbol. I felt deeply blessed for this miracle to be occurring in my own garden. Our gardener said what was happening was botanically inexplicable, but tragedy struck the following autumn when he pruned the rose bush and cut away the holy branch. I was devastated. In early spring of the following year, I stood by the bush and I asked Mary Magdalene, 'Are you going to bloom on my rose bush again this year?' She replied, as a silent speaking in my mind, 'I am going to bloom in you.'

When I reflected on the state of deep peace I had entered, and not come back from, during the session with David in March, I noticed that since then – without me doing anything different – my daily meditations had become altogether more sacred and holy. I still created an altar of sorts on my desk or on the kitchen table, with a candle and incense and sometimes sacred music. And I still followed the same naive pattern of simply sitting still on my chair. But now, when I meditated, it felt more like I was entering a state of deep prayer. In retrospect, I know that I was in a state of contemplation. Then, one evening in April, after a session with David during the day, I had my first vision during meditation.

When I began to meditate that evening, I had that same experience of crossing over to somewhere incredibly peaceful. Then I began crying quietly about a sadness that had come up during the craniosacral session. Somehow, with my eyes barely open, I was able to look into the tears that were sitting on my lower eyelids and eyelashes, and I was able to see a reflection of the dancing candlelight captured in my teardrops. As I looked at this amazing phenomenon, I then saw two separate petal-shaped forms of light standing still at the centre of the dancing light in my tears. And I don't know how, but I knew the petal-shaped lights were me and my womb twin, Aodhlagh.

As a child, I sometimes used to feel a kind of grief for the loss of someone close to me, but I never knew who it was. I felt an inexplicable loneliness, as if part of me were missing, and I often used to find myself searching for someone in the garden without knowing who. At the same time, from my earliest memory, I longed for and I pined for a twin sister. I longed for someone to be close to; someone like me, who experienced the world in the same strange way that I did.

When I was older, I began to have a better understanding of this longing, and realized that I may indeed have been searching for my twin, because by then I had intuited that I had a twin who had miscarried during my mother's pregnancy. In 2014, a clairvoyant had also confirmed to me that in utero I had actually been one of twins. Given that my grandmother had also died during my time in my mother's womb, I felt a bit hard done by. Two deaths in nine months and a mother in mourning: I later came to think that I myself was born mourning.

During that evening meditation I was entranced, watching the petal shapes of fire. The clairvoyant had given me my twin's name, but all I could understand of the name she gave me was the sound of the French words *et lá*. Only after meeting David did I finally make sense of the sound 'et lá', realizing that it could be spelled Aodhlagh, which is an Irish name, pronounced exactly the same way. It came to me in a flash of inspiration accompanied by a confirming current of electricity running through my whole body.

Aodhlagh has the same root as my own name, which in Irish is spelled Aodhammar. Aodhammar was the Celtic goddess of fire and also the name of one of the first Christian nuns in Ireland. The nun Aodhammar took her vows before St Patrick in the 5th century in a place called Laragh in County Wicklow, near the famous monastic site of St Kevin at Glendalough. I only discovered that Aodhammar had lived in a monastery in Laragh, the name I had chosen for my daughter, when my daughter was about two years old. It left me speechless.

When the vision of the petals of fire ended, even though I did not understand what had happened, the most accurate description that came to me when I tried to capture it in words for my journal was that I had 'crossed over' somehow or other to 'somewhere'. I had no idea where I had crossed over to, or even what I really meant by the phrase; I just had the strongest feeling that my spirit had done so. I had no language or understanding to really grasp what was happening.

I thought it was fascinating but treated it as a strange, abstract occurrence, with no real implications for me.

It did not cross my mind that I was developing a spiritual gift of any sort; nor did I think I was going mad, because there was a beauty and wholeness to what had happened, and I knew it all made sense in some frame of reference to which I just had no access. Once more, it was like hearing a foreign language that I did not understand – perfectly intelligible to those fluent in it, but alien to others. I did not interpret what had happened as belonging in any way to the category of mystical experience. I did not even spend time wondering whether other people were having similar experiences in meditation. I gave no thought to wondering if such a thing might happen again, but happen it did.

My next session with David was in the month of May. Immediately afterwards I went for a walk by the sea, and there – in broad daylight, in the middle of the day, while wide awake – I had a phenomenal, undeniable, whole, complete and staggering mystical experience. Even I could not fail to recognize it for what it was. There was no possibility of not understanding the experience as a full-blown mystical event. Such an event is often called a 'mountain-top experience', but for me it was a pier-end experience.

It happened as I was walking on the pier of Dún Laoghaire Harbour in Dublin Bay. The day was bright, the sky was blue, and on this midweek afternoon there were very few people about. As I walked, I was engaged in deep contemplation, reflecting not only on what had come up during the craniosacral session, but also on my growing understanding that Being itself is the divinity of God. I was reaching towards the idea that everything must belong in an intelligent and sacred whole, but it was still just an intuition; it had not properly taken shape in my mind. Yet, my thoughts weren't just philosophical ideas; they were also in my body as feelings of truth.

When I reached the end of the pier, I stood staring into the dark waters of the Irish Sea, and I began visualizing the sea at its deepest depths and marvelling that, no matter how deep the water goes, nor how far it stretches, it is still one sea. Nowhere can a point of divide be found anywhere in the world's oceans; and what is more even than that – the sea and all of creation are also one. I felt myself almost physically pulled into this visualization of the indivisibility of all creation.

And with that feeling came an immediate, spectacular revelation in my mind – a sudden, radical, powerful understanding of the concept that *all is one*. Instantly, I understood at the deepest imaginable level that *everything belongs in a deep, deep, deep connectedness*. I suddenly understood existence, and I *felt* my understanding with my whole being. I was electrified by this powerful '*felt*' understanding of the essential connectedness of everything that exists to everything else. I *felt* the connection in my own self, not just in my mind but in my body, and with my whole being. I knew and *felt* myself to be 'one' with everything that exists. It was phenomenal. I knew I had accessed the whole truth of existence. At last, I understood life!

I was so joyous, and I wanted to celebrate this amazing breakthrough in understanding. In awe, I said to myself, *You would expect fireworks when realizing such a thing.* And as I said those words, I felt what I can only describe as spiritual fireworks exploding inside my head. My hair was standing on end, my body felt as if a powerful current had brought it to life for the first time ever, I had goose bumps all over and my head felt as if it were on fire with joy. The whole thing was unbelievable and indescribable.

I had been pondering God for most of my life, and here, suddenly, on Dún Laoghaire pier on an ordinary midweek afternoon, the central truth of existence – that we are all connected – had been revealed to me. And not just revealed in theory, but through a profound knowing and feeling of truth at the core of my being. It was a truth that I could never lose: that there is a deep, deep connection between everything; that despite the multiplicity and diversity, all is nonetheless one. I felt this understanding with my whole being. I was filled with wonder and joy. Yes, I had read of this truth in books; yes, I had heard it at Mass; yes, I had read it in the Bible and in my philosophy studies; but this was an understanding of a different order entirely. It went so deep into me that it penetrated the core of my being and at the same time it brought me into the core of Being itself.

I had moved beyond knowing with my mind to feeling at my depths the truth of what I now knew. I had moved beyond the space-time continuum. I had entered a place of higher knowing and being. I had encountered truth. This was a revelation. I knew that my understanding of life could never be the same again now that I had *lived* the experience of knowing and understanding the essential connectedness of all with All.

~

CHAPTER 5

LIGHT ON FIRE

*'In this birth God pours forth His light in such
a way that its richness floods the very ground
and essence of the soul until it overflows into
its powers, even to the outer person.'*

MEISTER ECKHART

By the summer of 2015, I was undeniably curious about all things spiritual and I was more mature in every way than I had been back in 2007. I no longer had any regard for the appalling advice of St John of the Cross and I was able to make my own assessment of my recent vision and the revelation on the pier. I knew that they were sacred.

At around that time, a friend told me about a spiritual teacher/ psychic called Catherine who did consultations via online video calls, so I signed up for a session in early June. I was greedy to know more about this new transcendental dimension that was opening up to me, and I was hoping to receive some guidance.

It was a powerful reading. Catherine spoke a lot about how everything is connected, about how God is always already here, and about how all is actually one. And remarkably, due to the mystical knowing I had received on the pier, I was able to understand all the beautiful things she said at the deepest possible level. It was not just poetry; I *knew* them to be true.

She spoke of how God is in the trees, and the flowers, and in other people. I understood this too, at a very deep level. I had encountered the same idea in the work of Schelling. He called it 'panentheism', which is the idea that everything has its being in God. The Greek *pan-en-theism* literally means 'everything-in-God'. I had loved this idea intellectually, but in the moment, as she spoke, I was able to have an embodied and lived experience of this truth. I had chills all over my body, and I felt that deep sense of awe that is triggered when we know we are hearing truth. I remembered the joy I had experienced during the revelation on the pier, and I knew that it had been a lived experience of what Catherine was describing to me.

She then guided me through a meditation, inviting me to imagine myself lying in a beautiful field.

I closed my eyes and pictured myself lying on the grass under a huge oak tree on the beautiful campus grounds of University College Dublin. The campus is opposite my old family home, and when I was growing up I had spent so much time playing there that it was like a second garden to me. As she guided me deeper into relaxation, I had a profound experience of feeling myself transfigure into light – not only me, but also the oak tree. We both changed form entirely and became light.

I was awed by the experience, and my feeling of awe continued long after the session was over. The next day, I had the strangest feeling that there was a flood of energy pouring out of me, primarily through the top of my head. It seemed as if my bodily frame could no longer contain who I was; I was too big for myself, and was energetically overflowing out of my body, as if bursting at the seams and exploding the limits of my physical body. My energy was just too much for me.

Since then, I have come to understand this experience as part of the energetic dynamic of the expansion of our consciousness. It is part of the embodied-energetic component of our spiritual birth, growth or awakening. It is the expression of the energy involved in moving from the level of the psyche and the intellect to the level of spirit. It is part of the felt-experience, and the embodied element, of breaking through to spiritual consciousness.

Two weeks later, on the evening of the summer solstice, I went for a walk by the river near my home. I was immersed in thinking of God, of these recent experiences, and of all that I was by then coming to understand about God as Being-itself. I felt such a powerful love for God but also a deep sadness at the desperate state of humanity – which is nothing other than God's own being.

Nature, including *us*, is what God is when God manifests as matter. We are the material manifestation of God. How can we live in such disharmony with each other if we all started out in the beautiful mind of God?

As I walked, I contemplated the reality that God is in the trees, and the grass, and the flowing river – and suddenly, I got it! The spiritual fire exploded once again in my head. I saw and understood how the trees were my brothers and the flowers my sisters, how the river was alive, and how the evening sky, the setting sun and every blade of grass was ablaze with its own divinity.

I walked for over an hour, and during that whole time I had burning insight after burning insight into how God was manifestly present to me, in nature and also *in me*! An incandescent spiritual fire blazed in my head and in my whole body. I was in private ecstasy. I felt I knew God intimately, and I felt how special I am to God – how special we all are to God.

Moreover, I had a wondrous *felt* sense of how everything around me – the trees, the birds, the other people out walking – are all one. I both understood it and *felt* it, as I had understood and felt, on the pier, the glorious connection between every imaginable part of nature – of how it is that we most sublimely and necessarily, all together, have our existence in God.

The wondrous scale at which I was feeling
God to be in everything surpassed ordinary
knowing in every imaginable way.

~

It was clear that I had crossed over into a new form of knowing and understanding. I could never unknow or unsee all that was being revealed to me. This summer solstice walk was clearly a threshold experience in my life.

In the weeks and months following this experience, I was filled with desire to understand how mystical experiences like this could even happen. It was wonderful to enjoy the experience, but I longed to know the metaphysics behind it. I wanted to understand more about it all so that I could share some insights and help other people to have the same experience – I wanted everyone to experience this. If they could, we would have world peace instantly.

Ultimately, as I was creating the guide to awakening that I share in Chapter 15, I realized that the felt-knowing that I had experienced on the pier – of the belonging of all to the all – and the felt-knowing I had experienced by the river – of the divinity of all existence – are actually definitive milestones on the path to awakening. They constitute stages five and six on my guide, and we discuss them in detail in Chapter 15.

Beyond even my desire for insights into the metaphysical questions, however, I also wished with every ounce of my being that I could stay in the mystical state for always – for it to become my constant state of being so that I could be one with the presence of God in the trees and the flowers and the river and the sky for my whole life. Why is the mystical experience only temporary? Why did this joyous insight into the true nature of reality not become my constant state of knowing? Why did I have to revert back to ordinary human consciousness? My curiosity was intense and I was filled with questions but I had very few answers.

I knew Heidegger had written that we cannot stay in the 'moment of authenticity', and that Meister Eckhart and many other mystics taught that the mystic cannot remain in the mystic state but must come back and share what she knows with others, but I longed nonetheless to have that mystical awareness as my constant state of being and knowing. There was simply no comparison between that heightened state-of awareness and ordinary life. Father Richard Rohr, of the Center for Action and Contemplation in Albuquerque, New Mexico, also teaches of the importance of balancing action and contemplation. He says that we must always move between the two states, and that is why he deliberately chose that particular name for his centre.

I began thinking about one of the oldest principles of philosophy, which is that 'like knows like'. This means that, for one thing to know another, there must be a likeness between them that enables meaningful connection, communication or understanding to occur. For a mystical experience to be possible, there must be something in us that is like God, otherwise it could not happen at all – not even once. I wanted to know what that 'something' was.

The fact that we *can* have a meaningful encounter with God means that we do share some common identity. This has been expressed in different ways over the millennia. Meister Eckhart, my favourite, phrased it this way: 'The eye with which I see God is the eye with which God sees me.' He also described the likeness between us and God as our having a 'divine spark' within us – that there is something divine in *us* which is the part of us that can know God.

It was amazing to know, through my experiences, that God is in everything and everything is in God – that we fundamentally belong to God as part of God. But I wanted to understand the metaphysics of how all this is true. I wanted to really *know* God. I wanted to hold the love of God in me and to let it flow through me to the people around me. I wanted everyone to experience this amazing knowing of our essential connectedness and our inherent divinity.

I read different accounts from various mystics about the spiritual exercises they say are necessary to reach the mystic state – such as moving through the seven 'mansions' of St Teresa of Ávila's 'Interior Castle'. But I had not, or at any rate not consciously, done anything like that to engender my spontaneous mystical experiences, so I knew there must be more to be known. I also read Dr Joe Dispenza's book *Becoming Supernatural*, which shares some of the neuroscience of what happens in the brain during a mystical event. But, thus far, I had read nothing that explained what it is in our *being* that enables a mystical experience to happen in the first place. What, in our spirit or our mind, makes possible this *higher felt-knowing* of the connection of all to All, and of the divinity of all of life?

In particular, I wondered how a finite human being could even have an experience of the Infinite – and this became the crux of my confusion and the question that guided my enquiries for the next five years.

I knew that God is not a being, and that somehow God is not separate from us – but I could not understand how. I knew that we derive *from*, are held *in* and are part *of* God – and that, somehow or other, it is wrong to think we are separate from God – but I could not understand how this was possible: how do finite beings belong to the ineffable and infinite God?

If we truly belong to God, then why do we not incarnate with the self-knowing that we *are* human-divine beings, just as Jesus incarnated with full consciousness of his divinity? Jesus said, 'I and the Father are One.' Why is this higher consciousness veiled from us, yet is revealed in mystical experiences?

> *If we too, like Jesus, come from Spirit,*
> *if we have our being in God before we*
> *incarnate, why does incarnation cause us*
> *to forget this truth about ourselves?*

A central teaching of Plato is that all knowing is 'remembering'; that everything we learn here is a remembering of what we knew before this life; and that our birth causes us to 'forget'. This concept of our forgetting engaged me deeply. Why is 'forgetting' part of the human experience and part of our design? In ancient Greece and Rome, everyone believed in reincarnation: Plato called it 'transmigration of souls'.

Plato argued that if we are to believe in the immortality of the soul after death, then we must necessarily believe the soul's immortality exists in the other direction too, namely, pre-incarnation. Immortality by definition cannot have a starting point. Christianity came to reject the prevailing belief in reincarnation, but it seems to me that it does not matter whether we believe in reincarnation or not, or whether we believe in Atlantis, Lemuria or Sirius, or whether we have one or multiple incarnations, here or elsewhere, because the exact same question arises for everybody: why do we 'forget' our inherent divinity?

In the Book of Kings of the Old Testament, God said to Jeremiah: 'Before I formed you in your mother's womb, I knew you.' This phrase had always touched me deeply without me ever properly understanding what it might mean. But after these many years of reflection, my deepest understanding is that we do each have conscious pre-existence in spiritual form before we incarnate, in the mind of God, in the womb of Christ. Once I had reached this understanding I then wanted, with all of my heart, to access that state of original knowing and consciousness. I wanted to know what I knew when I was still in the womb of God, and why I had to forget it in order to become human.

I was frustrated, and felt that I was asking the wrong questions. I could not fathom the relationship between God and humanity.

Why did we have to forget our essential nature as spiritual beings? For what purpose? How did it happen, when, and why? God as pure intellect cannot make a mistake, therefore there is no error in our design. That must mean it is we who have gone wrong. Have we done something wrong to produce this forgetful finitude that afflicts us so much? Even though I no longer believed in original sin, the mindset of presuming we had done something wrong to produce our forgetfulness and our brokenness was so ingrained in me that it was difficult to overcome it.

So, for a long time, I continued to work from this basic premise – that we had done something wrong that caused us to forget our essential divinity – until at last, a number of years later, it finally dawned on me – this is exactly the way it is meant to be. We suffer because we do not understand. What I came to realize is that the whole point and purpose of life is to move from the darkness of this not knowing into the light of knowing, and in doing so, we 'remember' our divinity. It seems that life is a gift we have so far failed to understand, and most of our suffering starts here. I am looking forward to elaborating further on this liberating and holistic idea when we get to Chapter 14.

But, back at that stage in my journey, I just knew that there was more to life than I had ever imagined possible and that it was a struggle to understand it. That an ordinary someone like me could have these mystical experiences showed me there was so much more to learn about life. I began to live these questions with my whole being. But I also wondered: was it my destiny to know that there *was* more to life but to be unable to understand it. Was I to accept this frustration, just as I had previously accepted other peculiarities about myself? I tried to accept it, tried not to let it eat me up, but I was frustrated by my finitude, by my inability to stay in the mystical state and to have the constant presence of God with me in my daily life. I wondered if the human experience was simply destined to be one of pain and frustration, but I could not bring myself to believe that God, which is nothing but love, could create such an experience for Its own children. Or is it *we* who create the pain and the frustration?

These and many more questions became my constant companions over the next number of years, during which some incredible answers slowly revealed themselves to me. But at that point I had just begun to get a sense that my self-knowing as a specific individual was getting in the way of the understanding I craved.

In mid-July, a couple of weeks after the solstice experience in the park, I read a beautiful book by Walter Makichen, called *Spirit Babies: How to Communicate with the Child You're Meant to Have.*

Walter had the gift of clairvoyance and healing; from a young age, he had encountered some beautiful and sacred visions, especially in his Catholic church during Mass. He had no intention of making a career from this gift; instead, he wanted to become a professor of English. He was pursuing a PhD in English at the University of California, Berkeley, when one day, a figure of 'shimmering white energy' spontaneously appeared in his room. The energy told Walter that he would not finish his studies but instead would begin healing other people. The white energy then said that Christ wanted to talk to Walter and, with that, the white figure was replaced by 'a figure all in gold... a floating shimmering golden energy'. Christ spoke to Walter about his future work, telling him that he had an affinity with children and that he would 'help many spirits enter this world'.

Even though I knew almost nothing about clairvoyance or energy healing, I found it remarkably easy to believe all that Walter shared. Maybe his academic background vouched for his credibility in my mind, I am not sure, but without hesitation I accepted his strange story with ease.

At the end of each chapter, Walter shares a guided meditation. This was serendipitous, because I was still doing my own simple daily meditations, and I had been thinking about looking for some guidance in the 'proper' practice or technique of meditation. Walter's meditations involve working with the chakras and chanting. I had no understanding whatsoever of chakras or energy work. My life context was the Christian West, and I had never been exposed to learning about chakras, which I now know derive from Hinduism.

I looked for the most general of Walter's meditations and found the Rainbow Meditation. It is described as a meditation that helps to clear out your chakra system and aura so that you can find out what you want for your life. Now, I did *not* set the intention to find out what I wanted for my life, because as far as I was concerned, I already knew my life plan: I was starting the MA in creative writing in September, then going to finish my novel and pursue my PhD studies in philosophy. Ultimately I planned to become a successful Irish writer. I was just looking for some guidance on meditative practices, but – little did I know – I was about to gain so much more.

One evening in July, I settled in at my desk to do the meditation. Golden light from the setting sun flooded my study. The Rainbow Meditation felt easeful, and incredibly simple. It involves imagining your in-breath pulling a different colour up into your body through the sole of your left foot, taking it up to the different chakra locations on the body, and then your out-breath takes it out again down through the right foot. There was no explanation of how the colours relate to different parts of the physical, emotional and spiritual body, so I had no preconceptions about what I was working on. I simply breathed in the colours in the sequence listed – in complete innocence and naivety.

I visualized coloured energy travelling up and down my body for each different chakra colour, and as I did this, I felt powerful energy building inside me. I was quite taken aback. I faced a split-second decision: I knew I could stop this strange experience from developing any further if I wanted to. I could just stand up, walk away and break the spell, so to speak. But as that thought flashed across my mind, I heard my inner voice saying, *I am held up by the white light, and I can stay for this.* I have no idea how I came to say such a thing, the meaning of which I barely understood – except that I sensed it was completely safe to let the experience continue, and I also knew that I would miss something absolutely amazing if I walked away. So, I went with it – once more surrendering to an experience that lay far beyond my intellectual understanding.

When I got to the seventh chakra on top of my head, suddenly – without the slightest warning, without any preliminary sign, with nothing to prepare me for it – I felt Jesus come to me in a blaze of fire.

My head exploded with that same holy fire I had experienced on the pier, and in the park on the summer solstice – only this time, it was staggering in its intensity and in its holiness. I felt Jesus' presence as a blaze of energy, as a sacred fire, all around my head. As soon as he came, he said to me, 'I AM The I AM.' I heard the words silently in my head with an inner hearing, but they were spoken with phenomenal majesty, as a king speaking to the whole world.

As I heard them with my mind, I was filled with a feeling of staggering and sublime holiness.

I knew with absolute certainty, as part and parcel of the experience, that this holy fire I felt blazing in me and all around my head was Jesus. I do not know how I knew it; I just did. I *felt* Jesus, but I did not see anything. It was not a physical seeing in any way. It was a feeling-knowing at the level of the higher mind – the supra-rational or the spiritual mind. I could *feel* the incredible holiness of his presence, and his intimate closeness to me. His light surrounded me, and I was utterly absorbed into the experience. Nothing I could ever see with my physical eyes could come close to the beauty, the power and the profundity of this inner experience and this inner knowing.

Then I heard myself spontaneously begin to chant inside my head, saying, *I am in love, with love I am.* I had never heard such a sentence before. My inner voice repeated it many times. I was enraptured and lost all sense of my own being, my own body and the room I was in. The whole world had faded from my awareness to the point of obliteration as I was drawn completely into this joyous experience of Jesus. I was consumed by his holy fire, and I became fire, too. All I could do was live the enormity and the intensity of what was happening to me.

Then the energy of Jesus' fire, his spirit, flowed into me, and my fire flowed into his fire. I will try to explain this with an image of two fountains of water: one bigger (Jesus), one smaller (me), beside each other, taking turns cascading our flow of water in and out of each other in a figure-of-eight, like a vertical infinity symbol. We flowed into each other several times in a beautiful, seamless dance of flowing fire. It was utterly blissful. I was ecstatic. Spiritual ecstasy is something that mystics have described since the very beginning. We often see them depicted in holy rapture in art. That is what I was experiencing.

Throughout it all, the holy fire blazed in my head, and on every new in-breath, a fresh wave of fire came pouring into me through the top of my head. I was in awe at what was happening, for the blessing and the sacredness of being visited by Jesus. It was a happiness beyond anything that could ever be experienced in ordinary life. I wanted with all of my heart and soul to give myself to Jesus. The ecstasy lasted about three or four minutes, and as it ended, all I could think to do was to say, 'I offer myself to you. I am yours to do with me what you will. I am the handmaid of the Lord. I will do your will.' I was burning alive with spiritual fire, and even now, as I am typing these lines, my head is burning again with that same sacred fire.

Gradually, the fire subsided and I no longer felt Jesus to be present, but I continued in the meditative state, awestruck. When the meditation did come to an end, I wrote everything down in my journal, offering my gracious thanks to God for such a stunning and powerful revelation. I knew with certainty it had been The I AM with me, around me, in me, crossing over into me, and me crossing into It.

When I use the phrase, 'The I AM,' I am referring to God. Christians believe that Jesus was the human incarnation of God. 'I AM That I AM' is the name God gave to Itself when Moses asked God for Its name during the episode of the burning bush. God, as fire, had spoken to Moses and told him to lead the Israelites out of their slavery in Egypt. When Moses asked for the name of this God who was giving these commands, God said, 'I

AM That I AM' and also said that this was the name by which
It was to be remembered by all generations.

I was in awe and deeply grateful for this sacred visitation. I did
not know that it was the first of a series of almost daily mystical
visions that would occur for me over the next two years.

Not surprisingly, I decided to do the Rainbow Meditation again
the next day. In my morning meditation, I felt the green chakra
at my heart space to be the most alive, and the chakras felt more
activated and energized the higher up my body I went. When I
got to the purple one in my forehead, it became highly activated;
I felt a strong tingling sensation, like very lively pins and needles
dancing inside my forehead – and in my naivety, I calmed it
down! I was alarmed; I thought I must be doing something
wrong for this to be happening. I had no clue that this chakra
was my third eye, my wisdom centre, and that I was in contact
with beautiful, supportive and holy energy.

In my evening meditation, I had another phenomenal experience.
I breathed in the various colours once more and, when I drew
the colour white to the top of my head, I immediately felt the
presence of God as a halo of white light around me. I felt Jesus
with me, and I was inspired to chant 'I am in love, with love I
am' again and again. Then I heard these following words being
spoken silently inside my head: 'The light of God shines in this
house.' I was hearing it and I was also spontaneously repeating
it as a silent chant.

With my inner eye, I could see that I was immersed in a white glow.

I lost all awareness of my physical self, the room I was in and the whole world. It lasted a couple of minutes, and as before, the experience slowly ended, and then I felt myself coming back to awareness of the ordinary world. A pale comparison would be to think of waking up from an exquisite dream and reorienting oneself to this lesser reality. As it ended, I must have been having a conversation with myself in my head about it all, because I heard a voice inside my head say, *Be quiet and listen.* Then I again heard, *The light of God shines in this house.*

I felt blessed beyond words for what had just happened. I kept repeating the phrase, 'The light of God shines in this house.' It became a mantra for me. I said it frequently throughout the day for a long time, and it brought me immediate comfort.

The following day, I did Walter's meditation for connecting with my guardian angel. Christians believe that we each have our own personal guardian angel who accompanies us in every moment of our lives. I followed Walter's guidance, and I immediately felt a holy presence high up in front of me in my study. My eyes were closed, but I sensed the presence, which was pure, tender and full of love. I took it for granted that this was my guardian angel. With great reverence, I silently asked for her name, and with my inner hearing I heard her say, *Andreia*. At first, I was confused. Had she said Andrew, or Andrea? But she repeated it very clearly: *An-dre-ia*. As soon as I received her name, I was given a chant: *The light of love shines in me.*

I also spontaneously started chanting, 'I am in love, with love I am.' As I repeated it over and over again, I understood that what was meant by the second limb – 'with love I am' – was 'with love I AM'. It meant God as love, so that what I was saying was, in fact, 'I am in love with God, which is love.'

Several months later, I was reading Plato's *Republic*, and in it I discovered that *Andreia* is listed by Plato as one of the four cardinal virtues. It is a Greek word that means 'appropriate courage and fearlessness'. I discovered this at a time when I greatly needed to find the courage required to go public about these astonishing mystical experiences. It was comforting to know that courage itself was with me in the form of my guardian angel, Andreia.

The next morning, I did my own version of meditating, which was simply to sit in silence with my eyes closed, and to be still. I felt a strong tingle for several minutes at the centre of my forehead – but I had no idea that it had any significance. I also received the following chants: *The healing light of Christ is here*; and again, *The light of God shines in this house.*

A couple of days later, I had an even more wondrous experience when I did another of Walter's meditations. This one involved clearing the seventh chakra above the top of one's head. This chakra is represented by the colour white. The meditation was designed to help women overcome the fear of pain in labour, or of dying in childbirth. My family was already complete so I knew that I would never be in labour again, but I had suffered immense fear during the births of both of my children. I was doing the meditation in the limited way I felt it could now help me: simply clearing the seventh chakra. I had no idea that, in Hinduism, the seventh chakra represents connection with divine consciousness and grace. I did not know that this must have been the reason why, in the preceding days, when I had breathed into the white chakra, Jesus and God had come to me.

Walter's meditation involved chanting some vowel sounds and then imagining drawing a white light up from the base of the spine to the top of the head; as one exhales, you imagine the white light radiating out of the top of your head.

As soon as I closed my eyes to begin the meditation, a new chant came to me: *I am in The I AM.* Then I felt my womb twin, Aodhlagh, and my guardian angel, Andreia, very close to me. I began the steps of the meditation and immediately felt spiritual fire burning in my head. I heard myself silently repeating, 'I am in The I AM.'

Every breath I took during the meditation drew more fire into me through the top of my head. I 'saw' pure white light above me. Then, in a split second, my spirit left my body and was now in that white light. My spirit became one with the white light, fusing entirely with it. I was out of my body, in the spirit world, and I was *in* The I AM. This, of course, is not a 'place' by any measure; it is a state of mind, or a state of being. It is beyond all possible description, outside space and time. I was in the pure being of God. I felt eternal wonder. I thanked God from my deepest depths for the sacredness of this experience.

> *I knew God was with me, and I knew that I was in God.*

As it ended, I had such a strong sense that there was something that I was supposed to do, but I had no idea what it was. I said, 'I will go back and do my job, whatever it is.' Then I felt the Holy Spirit flowing into me like a river of fire through the top of my head. Instinctively, I knew that from now on, the Holy Spirit would be with me much more than it ever had been with me before. As the experience of being in God ended, I sensed my seventh chakra closing and, as it did, white light was flowing into me. I presumed it was the Holy Spirit flowing into me, to stay with me. I felt incredibly beautiful in myself, as if my whole inner being was now shining white light. I was overflowing with joy.

After the meditation, I had a strong sense that I was ready to do my work, even though I had no idea what that work was. I also had a strong sense that my destiny was coming ever closer, but once again, I had no idea what that destiny might be.

There was no real need to know what these things meant; everything that was happening to me recently was so unutterably strange and beautiful and holy that I did not try to examine the details. When I think of how frightened I had been in 2007, when I read St John of the Cross's words about how experiences such as these could come from the devil, it makes me wonder why the Church would ever try to steer people away from such holy encounters.

In late July, I did the Rainbow Meditation again and had yet another stupendous experience. When I reached the white colour above my head, I immediately left my body and became lost in God. I started to feel myself merge with the presence of God. And then, miraculously, I was no longer different to God; rather, I felt myself to be *in* God, *as part of God*. I felt myself to be absolutely nothing, just as God is pure no-thing-ness. My nothingness was in God's nothingness. It was amazing. I had lost all sense of my own separate identity. Aedamar was subsumed into God and no longer had any separate existence.

Then I began to chant, silently and spontaneously, 'The breath of God is in me.' I also heard myself saying inside my mind, *The Breath of the Holy Spirit of Christ is in me*. And I had a deep sense that from now on, I would feel the Holy Spirit breathing in me, as me, with me and for me.

The intensity of this encounter with God then subsided – by which I mean that my sense of being one-with-God began to fade, and I came back to my own separate identity as Aedamar.

It is difficult to explain. The holiness and the strangeness of the experience frightened me a little, and I spontaneously called to Archangels Michael and Raphael to be with me and to protect me. Archangel Michael is known in Christianity as the Archangelic Protector and Raphael is known as the Healer.

Then I felt the energy or the power of the Holy Spirit pouring into me through the top of my head like a river of fire. With every breath, a feeling of fire came rushing into me through the top of my head, setting my head and my body ablaze with holiness. I drew in about 10 breaths of what I can only describe as pure spiritual fire.

I prayed that I might do the will of God alone, and that I be guided in God's will by the Holy Spirit. I thought of Pentecost, which is the Christian feast day that celebrates the event of the Holy Spirit descending onto the disciples as tongues of fire and bestowing on them many gifts of speech. I felt the exact same thing was happening to me – or, if I was wrong about that, I at least had a whole new understanding of what they had experienced. I *felt* what it was like for the Holy Spirit to flow into someone, even if I might not be allowed to believe it had actually happened to me.

Afterwards, I sat in awe at my desk and had a staggering realization: we are all *in* God. God is not something that *we* have in us: rather, God has us in *It*.

I was electrified by this new understanding. We cannot contain God, even as a thought. God exceeds all possibility of our knowing God. We are held, maintained and known *by* God. We must not try to know God by grasping after God and seeking to know God as a concept. Instead, we must approach God as Levinas advised: not by seeking to know, but by seeking to be in relation with God and by seeking to experience God.

I felt that, at last, I understood what God was: pure light, pure love, eternally holding us and loving us as Its own self. I also knew that what had been revealed to me is what God is offering to every single human being, every single day of our lives. And I realized that what I had just experienced *is* the Promised Land. *This* is what awaits us when we learn to live as the beings of light and love that we are. *This* is the Second Coming, *this* is heaven on Earth.

⁓

CHAPTER 6

A SOUL ON FIRE

*'Be who God meant you to be and
you will set the world on fire.'*
St Catherine of Siena

In August of that same year, 2015, we took our summer holidays out beyond Clew Bay in County Mayo, on the Atlantic coast of the west of Ireland. We rented a house on the stunning coastline of this breathtakingly beautiful, mythical and mystical place.

The vast horizon and the wild landscape of the west coast of Ireland gives a tremendous feeling of freedom to the soul. Its boundless emptiness spreads across the sea to America in one direction and across green fields dotted with ancient ruins in the other. The holy mountain of St Patrick, Croagh Patrick, presides majestically over it all, reaching to the heavens with its grey stony peak. This is the only place on Earth I know that is primal enough for my soul to expand to its natural size. It spreads itself across the wild expanse of sea, earth and sky and I feel that I truly come home to myself here, in the untamed landscape of my foremothers and -fathers.

It was a beautiful summer, the sun blazed in the sky, and we were happy and attuned to the peaceful rhythm of the ocean's slow tide. I was immersed in writing my novel, reading and wondering deeply about the amazing experiences I had been having in my recent meditations. My biggest interest was the question of God and creation, and why creation seems to have gone so desperately wrong.

Walking in nature became a holy experience for me that summer. Since the mystical experience on the pier in April, and in the park on the summer solstice, I had developed a whole new relationship with nature, and I could easily perceive it to be alive with its own divinity. I had a new awareness of its inherent spirituality and sacredness. The sun shone magnificently, the sky was a beautiful blue, the ocean a shimmering radiance and the grass of the fields was lush green – a kaleidoscope of joyous colours, reflecting my happy mood.

When I went for a daily walk by the ocean, or on the little boreens marked out by ancient stone walls, I was filled with thinking of the divine, and very quickly it began to happen that the holy fire I was experiencing during my meditation practice now began to blaze in me as I walked, too. As soon as I turned my mind to God, fire burned joyously in my head and often in my whole body. I now sensed God in everything: the sea, the sand, the sky, the hedgerow, the grass, the flowers growing wild on the side of the roads, the farm animals and in me. I sensed everything to be in God, and God to be in everything: God in all and all in God. I felt the divinity of our original creation, and I felt the unbreakable belonging of creation to its creator.

I felt that I was now 'home' in God; and when one arrives home to God in their knowing and in their being there is nowhere else to go and there is nothing else to know. That is the Omega point, when we have actualized and embodied the knowing of our own divinity. In retrospect, I know that what I was experiencing was actually the transformation of my consciousness into a consciousness of the divinity of all creation – which is stage six of the awakening process that we explore in Chapter 15.

Life became incredibly holy.

By this time, I was frequently having the experience during meditation that I described in my diary as 'feeling that I had stepped out of myself and into God'. I did not yet know to describe this as an experience of my spirit leaving my body, because it was not as intense or dramatic as the experience I described earlier, when my spirit most decidedly *did* leave my body. These experiences were less powerful or less intense, so I used that quite rudimentary description of stepping out of myself and into God. But I did fully understand that the only thing beyond any finite being is the Infinite itself, or God. To leave one's finitude is to step into the Infinite.

On the 13 August, Mary the Divine Mother came to me for the first time in meditation. As I meditated, I felt the white light of Christ shining in me. The chant I received was, 'I AM in me.' Jesus spoke to me, and in speaking he gave me these words to say: 'The holy light of Christ shines in me. The holy light of Christ burns through me. The Word burns in me and with this I must set the world on fire. My future is clear: it is to contribute to the spiritualization of the world. It is time for us to move beyond the spoken Word to the Word of fire. Let those who burn now come together to spread the fire of Christ. Let those who I am destined to meet now enter my life. I trust the Lord my God.'

As those beautiful sentences were completed in my mind, Our Lady then came to me and said, 'The way that we speak to you is through the fire that burns in you. That is how we speak to you. The fire that burns in you is the Word, and you must set fire to the world with it.' Afterwards I wrote it all down in my diary, and as usual, I added my thanks to God and now also to Mother Mary. I wrote, 'Amen. I wait for guidance.' I knew the Word they were referring to was the Word as used in the Gospel of St John to signify God, the Logos or Christ.

The next day I went for a walk on the beach, feeling awed by all that was happening, and especially by what Mother Mary had said to me about how heaven speaks to me in the holy fire and that I am to 'set the world on fire with it'. I wondered how I could possibly do such a thing – what did it even mean? What was I to do?

As I asked those questions of myself, suddenly Mother Mary spoke to me again, inside my mind, and she said with stunning clarity, 'Give back all that you have received by describing it.' Well, there was an answer: I was to describe the experiences. I was not being asked to come up with some world-changing mystical theology. I was not being asked to split the atom. I was being asked to describe my experiences, simple as that.

It could not have been any clearer: give back all that you have received by describing it!

I felt great peace. This was something I could do – indeed, I was already doing it by recording everything that happened in my diary. It seemed all I had to do was get my diaries published, although I was under no illusion about the difficulty of getting published, even when God has directed the book to be written. But on the many, many occasions when I have fallen into hopeless doubt about this new path I am pursuing, the hundreds of times I have lost my confidence, the innumerable days I have lost faith in the whole project, and the countless times my courage has failed, I remind myself of this crystal-clear instruction: that all I am being asked to do is to describe what happened.

On the last day of our holiday, I was very sad to be leaving this beautiful place where the divine was manifestly present to me, all of the time – not just in meditation but everywhere in nature. The thought of returning to the noisy city was breaking my heart because I presumed that I would lose the phenomenal mystical connection to God that I had been enjoying in this special place. How could God reach me, or how could I reach God, on the busy city streets?

On that last evening, I went for a walk on the beach. A spectacular sunset detonated from below the horizon line, sending a blaze of fiery colours – red, orange, pink, gold, blue and purple – exploding slowly across the darkening sky. I felt the beauty of it with my whole being, and my body burned with holy fire as I watched this celestial work of art. But there was also grief in the knowledge that I had to leave this divine beauty behind. I stayed there until the night was pitch black, and I was in tears as I left the beach, thinking I would not feel the majesty and the joy of God's fire so richly and powerfully in me again, until we returned there the following year. I was praying what I thought was a hopeless prayer: that the daily fire would live on in me in Dublin.

Leaving the beach was like leaving a dying loved one for the last time, knowing the desperate finality has come, and knowing I would never see them again. I felt that I was losing God, presuming this would be the end of the mystical experiences in nature. It felt as though my heart was breaking. Driving home to Dublin the next day, I was very sad. My whole being wanted to stay by the ocean so that I could commune freely with God. I felt desolate – but what I did not yet understand is that once a person is awakened to this majestic level of higher knowing, sensing and feeling, it cannot be lost. It does not depend on our location in the physical geographical world; it depends on how we are in our being. All that matters is the state of awareness that we choose to pursue.

I was soon to realize that the beauty of communing with God depends only on our willingness to adopt the appropriate reverential state of mind and being, and on our willingness to let it happen. It is a gift; it is something we receive – all we need to do is ready ourselves to receive it.

When I got back to Dublin, my burning awareness of God's presence in nature did indeed continue and I was thrilled. On my very first walk by the river, I had the joy of the sacred fire burning in me for the entire walk. I realized there was actually a pattern or a form to what happened. The way it worked was that I would take a very conscious breath, inviting God to enter me, seeking to draw God into me on that breath, and miraculously, I would feel the holy fire rushing in through the crown of my head. I would feel holy fire suffusing my whole head, and sometimes it would flow down into my body, and then I would burn in a silent joy to know the presence of God in me. When I was on fire in this way, I then perceived the divinity of nature all around me. It was as if I had new eyes with which to see. I saw that the grass and the earth and the trees and the sky were alive with life. I felt the life force in nature, and it felt it in me, too. We were deeply connected to each other and able to communicate our joy at this shared knowing that all is divine.

*It crossed my mind, of course, that nature never
loses its self-knowing as being alive with life.*

It is no surprise that the breath is the channel the divine uses
to enter us; to come into our consciousness and into our bodily
being, coming in as sacred fire that we miraculously feel burning
in us – without it actually burning us. Our breath is the source
of our life, our breath is the breath of life itself. My guess is that
when I feel the fire of God coming into me on my in-breath, the
burning I feel is the same burning that mystics have described
for millennia; the same fire that entered the apostles, female and
male, on Pentecost; the same fire that Moses encountered in the
burning bush that did not burn.

The breath is central to all spiritual practice, whether it be to
calm the body in prayer, meditation or contemplation, or as a
foundational technique of yoga that connects the practitioner
with God. The breath has been used by shamans of indigenous
cultures since ancient times to enter altered states of
consciousness and to connect with God or the Gods. The breath
is sacred to ancient religions and wisdom systems; it is known as
chi in China, *prana* in India, *ruach* in Hebrew, *aloha* in Polynesian
culture and *spiritus* in Latin, meaning both breath and spirit.

It is now also being used in much psychospiritual therapy:
for example, Stanislav Grof recently brought us holotropic

breathwork as a way to induce altered states of consciousness in order to access higher knowing. Our breath expressly connects the physical-material to the spiritual. Breath is sacred. The simplicity of being able to connect with God through conscious breathing is just astonishing.

By this stage, I was able to observe the steps of what happens to me in the sacred experiences I have when I meditate. When I have stilled my body and mind completely, when I have invoked the divine, or Jesus or Mary Magdalene, then I can actually feel an energetic shift as a slight 'choke' or change in my breathing, and when that happens, I cross over to God consciousness. I become nothing to myself. I become subsumed into God's own identity and I no longer exist as, or for, myself. I hand myself over to God.

I had also begun to accept that my life at its deepest expression was now devoted to God. I had a profound sense of wellbeing in my inner self, and I made a private commitment to be for God and to offer myself up to the will of God, knowing now that the will of God is only ever love. I aligned my will with the will of God and committed myself to living for love. I had a deep sense of inner peace and I felt that all was very well in the way that Jesus had assured Julian of Norwich: 'All shall be well, and all shall be well, and all manner of things shall be well.'

I privately decided to proceed on my path, wherever it may lead, believing deeply that it was a divinely ordained path. I sensed that God had opened my spiritual ear in order for me to hear

God. In my naivety, however, I did not realize that these private commitments I was making to God would become my public life. I still thought that I could keep my spiritual life separate from my public life. How wrong I was.

~

CHAPTER 7

A SPIRITUAL EMERGENCE

'Become Who I AM.'
VOICE OF GOD

Now that the extraordinarily holy experiences were continuing on a daily basis in meditation and in nature, I had some serious thinking to do. Clearly, this was not a passing phenomenon or a 'trick of the light', but an established, sustained and continuing life experience that I needed to engage with to try to understand what was really going on. It was no longer feasible to consider these as random, inexplicable, unconnected, meaningless experiences. One part of me was completely aware that these were full mystical experiences on a par with those I read about in mystical literature. Another part of me, however, could not take the next logical step in reasoning, because that would involve me saying I was a mystic – and that was not something I was able to do. I could not make such a claim, even in the privacy of my own mind.

I was also deeply aware that the mystics I read about practised absurd levels of self-denial, purgation, asceticism and prayer, and insisted that this type of practice was necessary for God to deign to visit a human. And since I was doing almost none of those practices except prayer, how could God be visiting me? I was in deep confusion and I had no one to turn to. How could I tell anyone about the experiences I was having without them thinking that I had gone completely mad?

I did consider the possibility that I *had* gone mad: that I was delusional; that what was happening did not mean I was a mystic; that somehow I was drawing the wrong conclusion. Yet, at the end of every exploration of my sanity, I came back to the simple fact that what was happening was in fact happening and I was not imagining it. I suffered mental anguish and turmoil – who would not feel turmoil in these circumstances? I knew exactly the reaction and the reception I would receive if I told anyone: they would think I was insane. And I knew from my career as a lawyer how dangerous it can be to get sucked up into the mental health system so that all autonomy is taken from you. I imagined that, once someone had been deemed insane, every statement – however sane – could be twisted into further proof of insanity. I also probably had a residual fear around the burning of women at the stake during the Middle Ages for supposedly unorthodox spiritual practices. My guess is that they were mystics that the Church could not tolerate.

So, I had no impulse to look for help; I was keeping it to myself for my own good. I was scared to tell my husband, scared to tell my friends, scared to tell my family, scared to speak to a professional counsellor. And I thought it was outside the remit of what I could reasonably bring to my craniosacral therapist – I did not yet understand his role as the guardian of my awakening.

Within my mind I held two very different possible life trajectories: was my original life plan to become a novelist still viable, or would I make the leap into the dark to follow this incredibly strange sense of being 'called' to follow a spiritual path? On the outside, my life looked completely the same; but on the inside, I was fluctuating between deep soul peace and deep soul confusion.

An unlikely source of support, if not exactly comfort, was available to me from the full year I had spent in psychoanalysis in 2006–07, when I attended sessions three times a week. This had given me important skills and knowledge I could draw upon. I was deeply familiar with processing anguish of the soul, the dark night of despair, the sense of complete abandonment by all of humanity, and of being alone in the abyss with no help from anyone except my dispassionate psychoanalyst. I also knew that I had navigated and survived far worse mental anguish during my postnatal depression. So, I had a degree of experience when it came to the self-questioning and the self-analysis required to explore what was happening to me.

By then, I had also learned the painful lesson that true maturity is characterized by personal responsibility and self-reliance. I was undergoing an advanced lesson in applied maturity, delivered with the ferocity of a tornado in my mind. I was on my own; no one else was coming to help. I took vague comfort from knowing that my experiences mirrored exactly the reports from mystics throughout history. If they were not mad, maybe I wasn't either. If they survived to tell their stories, maybe I would, too.

Compounding this confusion and turmoil was the fact that, as August proceeded, I began to have a strange feeling in my body – a feeling that I wanted to get 'out of myself'. I did not understand it. It was similar to the feeling of 'overflowing' that I had experienced after the solstice, but much stronger. Then it developed into a feeling that it wasn't actually *me* trying to get out of myself, but that *something* was coming out of me, or maybe through me – not something physical, obviously, but that an energy or a feeling was trying to come through me. Much as I had learned to live with the moods and the longing, I learned to live with this feeling, too, doing my best to understand it. Some days, I admit, I did wonder if I would end up in a psychiatric hospital after all. I knew that what I was experiencing was immensely holy, but I still had to question myself. Maybe I *was* actually going mad and losing my grip on reality. What I did not yet know was that this energy I felt coming through me was once again the energetic component of the transformation of consciousness being expressed in my body, as a felt, embodied and lived experience.

This is the paradox of spiritual awakening – it happens in the body.

My greatest resource, as ever, was more reading. I explored highly regarded academic works on mysticism across all faiths, especially those examining the subject through the lens of philosophy. Of particular help was *Phenomenology and Mysticism* by Anthony J. Steinbock, a professor of philosophy at Southern Illinois University in Carbondale. His book explored the phenomenon of mystical experience as reported by mystics from Islam, Judaism and Christianity. Reading these texts was a comfort. I was greedy for the wisdom of great minds discussing the exact experiences I was having. Ultimately, I was reassured that I was not going mad, but was instead incredibly blessed, and I needed to face up to this reality.

The following year, I read works by Stanislav Grof, John Perry and others in the field of transpersonal psychology. Through this research I finally came upon the distinction between a spiritual emergency and a spiritual emergence. The symptoms of both can be similar and are frequently confused by supposed experts. As a result, someone going through a *spiritual emergence* often ends up in a psychiatric ward, wrongly diagnosed as having a *spiritual emergency* – or in other words, a psychosis.

Reassured and comforted by all that I read, I realized it was no longer an option to stand, as it were, apart from what was happening to me. To receive such a gift was not a random happening in my life, not something that happened in my spare time; rather, it pervaded my whole consciousness, and my whole way of being in the world. I needed to consider accepting it and finding a way of integrating it into my life. The bald question was: was I a mystic? And if so, what was I going to do about it? I also had to balance my reluctance to claim the mystic gift against what I deemed would be deeply shameful and regrettable – to reject it.

～

CHAPTER 8

I AM, IN LOVE

'Speak, Lord, your servant is listening.'
BOOK OF SAMUEL

Throughout the summer months of 2015, two different lines from the Bible kept spontaneously announcing themselves in my head. The first was from the Old Testament, Book One of Samuel, 'Speak, Lord, your servant is listening.' It often popped into my head as I walked in nature or began a meditation, and each time, as I prayed the line, a holy fire would explode in my head. The other was a line from a hymn quoting Isaiah: 'Here I am, Lord, is it I, Lord? I have heard you calling in the night; I will go, Lord, if you lead me, I will hold your people in my heart.' This one in particular used to produce phenomenal fire in my head when I sang it silently in my mind. I thought it was ironic that both quotes involved hearing, given that my spiritual journey began precisely through my seeking help for deafness in my left ear.

On 30 August, I had a particularly beautiful experience in meditation. With my inner seeing I saw and felt myself to be in a white light that I understood was the light of the Holy Spirit, and also in golden light, which I knew to be God. Some beautiful chants came to me, again spontaneously, which opened up a new level of understanding for me. This was one of the chants:

I am in Love
I live in Love
Armed with the Light of Christ, I am here to do God's will.

Later that day, the following chant came to me. It was spontaneously spoken in my mind:

I am in the Light of Christ.

The new understanding that opened up was the double sense in which these phrases could be understood. Let me explain by using the chant, 'I am in love.' In the first place, it can be a simple statement of physical presence: I am *in* the presence of love. But I also now understood the much more powerful meaning available if we understand the words 'I am' in the sense of Being. Then, it can mean: *I have my being* when I am in the presence of love. This was very exciting for me – to realize that I was being told that I have my being in love; which essentially means that I only come into my true and fullest being when I am in the presence of love. And I also understood that I can *only* have my true being in love, since love is the source of all Being. God as love gives me my being, and my being is maintained in love, by love.

The same interpretations were equally available for the second chant: 'I live in love' – meaning either: I live *in the presence of* love; or, and again much more powerfully: I *owe* my life to love; I *only truly live* when I live in love; without love I do not live, I do not exist, I have no being. The same interpretation applied also to the last chant, so that I understood it to mean: I *only have my true being* when I am in the light of Christ.

This distinction goes to the core of how we live our lives. For the most part, we live at the first level of superficial presence rather than at the deeper level of Being. We express ourselves at the finite and surface level instead of at the deeper level of Being. When we do live at the deeper level of Being, we are opened to the whole infinite realm of God, of vast consciousness and intelligence, to Being-itself, and we recognize our true belonging to that whole.

To live at the level of the material-physical-egoic is not true living at all. Living at the surface level is what Heidegger called living through 'idle chat' as opposed to living in authenticity and being in relationship with Being-itself. The distinction also expresses the lesson Jesus came to teach – that we must die to the concerns of the ego in order to live at the level of spirit. It is utterly transformative to live at the level of being and spirit. This was what was now happening to me: my consciousness was expanding; the boundary between my finitude and the Infinite was dissolving. The surface level of life was no longer enough for me – it never had been. I was now plugged in at the level of Being, and I needed to reorder my life to reflect this new deeper awareness of the inherent divinity of all in All.

Later that day, I read a beautiful reflection in Iyanla Vanzant's book *Until Today!* It was about allowing the Holy Spirit to guide us into the next step of our personal growth and spiritual development. I made a commitment to let that happen. As I reflected on Iyanla's words, I fell to thinking about the gift that is often called 'the sight', and wishing that I had it. In my naivety, I thought that clairvoyance, or being a psychic, was a necessary component of the mystical gift. I thought that, if I had the sight, it would act as confirmation that I was in fact becoming a mystic. As I daydreamed about having the sight, a voice in my head spoke very gently to me, saying, *You do. You can feel things no one else can feel. You see in a different way.* I was thunderstruck. It felt like a most holy communication.

That evening I fell into confusion about what was happening to me. I was upset and I prayed a confused, even desperate prayer, begging once and for all for clarity. I asked, *Dear Jesus, am I a mystic? It seems too much for me to claim. But if it is your will for me, then I will accept that I am a mystic.*

Instantly my whole body burned alive and Jesus spoke inside my mind, saying, *It is your prize, Aedamar.*

I was overjoyed. The intimacy of hearing Jesus say my name made me feel incredibly loved. I was deeply touched. It was the only time my name was ever spoken in all of my holy experiences. And to think anyone would deserve a prize for finding God – the prize, of course, *is* God. To know God is the highest possible level of knowing, and when it happens, it is felt as a burning joy, as the highest imaginable pleasure and happiness. To know God is to experience God. It is the joining together of the knower with the known, which philosophy defines as the true experience of knowing. It is the question the poet W.B. Yeats asks in *Among School Children*: 'How can we know the dancer from the dance?' In mystical terminology, it is called 'union with the divine', or becoming one with the divine. Julian of Norwich called it 'Oneing'.

> *I then wrote in great happiness in my journal, thanking God for this stunning gift. I wrote: 'I am in God. I am in love.'*

The next morning when I meditated, I felt myself glowing in God. I saw different colours with my inner eye and was ablaze with holy fire. Then I saw gold and white light. A chant came to me:

I see by the Light of Christ.
I hear by the Light of Christ.
I am by the Light of Christ.

I was burning beautifully, and white light poured into my head.

Later that day, by astonishing serendipity, I started reading a beautiful book called *Mysticism in English Literature* by Caroline Spurgeon. The book picked up on this exact theme of being able to feel what others cannot feel. In it she described four categories of mystics: mystic philosophers; religious mystics; nature mystics; and mystics of love and beauty, who are primarily poets. Spurgeon then wrote that, whatever their differences, '[mystics] all alike agree... in one passionate assertion... that unity underlies diversity.' She argued that the 'basic fact of mysticism... [is] founded upon an intuitive or experienced conviction of unity, of oneness, of alikeness in all things.'

I was so relieved to read this simple but profound definition of what a mystic is. To then read the following words, about the role of *feeling* in the mystic experience, gave me great joy:

> *Finally, the mystic holds these views because he has lived through an experience which has forced him to this attitude of mind. This is his distinguishing mark, this is what differentiates him alike from the theologian, the logician, the rationalist philosopher, and the man of science, for he bases his belief, not on revelation, logic, reason, or demonstrated facts, but on feeling, on intuitive inner knowledge.*

As I read these words, I was awestruck, and a rainbow flashed at the corner of the page beside the word *feeling*. My head was on fire. If *feeling* was the mark of a mystic, then maybe I was a mystic.

I felt enormous relief, at last, to have this simple account of what a mystic is. It took away my anxiety that I was making some grandiose claims about myself. It brought it all down to Earth in a very simple way – that a mystic quite simply has lived the experience of the 'oneness of all', has lived it as a *felt experience* as opposed to having mere theoretical knowledge of it, and it has given them a new understanding of the world. This was such a relief. It was nothing that the poets have not been writing about since the very beginning. Being a mystic was something to be celebrated rather than feared, something to be valued rather than be ashamed of. Relief washed through me like a cold drink on a hot day. There was no need to be scared. For the first time, I felt that maybe I could accept what was happening to me.

⌒

CHAPTER 9

I AM THE I AM

'They are the sons and daughters of Life's longing for Itself.'
KHALIL GIBRAN, ON CHILDREN

It was now September 2015, which meant it was back to school for my kids and back to college for me. I was starting my MA in creative writing with a confused heart because I had a strong intuition that my future lay in spiritual writing rather than in the fiction I was actively pursuing. The career path I had mapped out for myself as a future novelist was fading from view in favour of this incredibly unclear possible path forwards. I had no idea what I could contribute to the world of spiritual writing – and therefore how I could possibly build the career I needed to build – yet I felt that was where I was being called.

Over and above those practical concerns, my ego also had a problem.

My degree results were out, and I learned that I had graduated with a double first, and had taken first place in philosophy at University College Dublin and nationally across the five universities of the National University of Ireland. The Schools of English and of Philosophy had both invited me to proceed straight to PhD studies. My ego therefore feared that if I were to go down the road of writing spiritual books about mysticism, I would lose all academic and literary credibility and those paths would become closed to me.

I was deeply confused. How could it be that I had extricated myself from the rat race of a legal career, fought the battle with my ego to enter my authenticity, retrained in a deeply soulful discipline aligned with my true self, and got all of my skittles lined up for the first time ever in my life – only for it all to be taken away from me to follow an intuition that I was to become a spiritual author writing about God knows what?

On 10 September, I did Walter's meditation for connecting with my guardian angel. I felt a beautiful burning sensation throughout, and my angel said to me, *We hold you in our arms. Your light will shine.* Then beautiful light energy poured into my head and I heard, *The golden light of Christ fills you. You will shine. You have done great work for Christ and you will do more. Christ has a special place in His heart for you.* I was awed by this astonishing message, and incredibly grateful. It was beautiful to hear. My deep felt-knowing was that: *I am love and All is love.*

In late September, I was reflecting on the fact that I had not experienced one of my moods for quite a few months, which surprised me. I calculated that the last mood was the one that lasted from December to March, when I had entered deep peace during the session with David. I was confused as to why they had suddenly stopped. Now that I was at last able to understand what was going on, able to enjoy the meaningfulness of the moods, where had they gone? Now I knew them as a kind of 'portal' into another level of consciousness, and I was fascinated and absolutely ready to explore further. For 46 years I had failed to understand them, yet now that I did, they had stopped. I read back over my journal looking for some insight, and there I struck gold.

I re-read my account of entering, and not returning from, the state of deep peace during the March session with David, and in particular my subsequent feeling that 'the mood itself seemed satisfied with itself, that it… had achieved in me what it had wanted to.' Suddenly I realized that what had been achieved was that I had been moved from the moods to mysticism.

This finally helped me to understand something I had vaguely intuited all along: that the moods were some form of preliminary preparation for mysticism. Now it struck me as a truth that they had indeed been preparation for the sacred experience of being brought into the presence of the divine. They had functioned as a practice run of sorts, acclimatizing me to the movement between the realms. Whereas I had been passive in the movement of the moods, I can actively surrender to God through meditation and contemplation.

I was thrilled, but there was even more to come. As I sat by the fire in my study that Saturday evening, reflecting on these things and truly racking my brain to try to understand, a further stunning realization began to form in my mind. But before it could take shape, I became hyperaware and sensitive to the energetic plane. I felt a strong sense of premonition that something big was coming in. My thinking slowed down, and I felt the world slow down, as if time itself were standing still to open up a sacred space for the understanding that was coming to me. Very slowly, my thoughts began to connect, like pieces of a jigsaw coming together all by themselves. In slow motion, I understood that whatever it was that used to draw me into the mood; whatever it was that was longing in me; whatever it was that *I* was longing for; the 'place' of peace that I was brought into; the meaning I intuited but could not understand – they were all nothing other than God Itself. Awestruck, I wrote in my journal: 'The "thing", by the way, is God!!!!!!!!!!!!!!!!!!!!!!!'

This breakthrough made me ecstatic. It helped me to see the connection between Heidegger's mood of detachment that brings us into relation with primordial Being and the mystical experience of being brought into the presence of the Divine by the Divine. I realized that they constituted two phases of the one experience, or two levels of understanding of the one experience, or two sides of the same coin – one secular, one mystical. For my entire life, I had lived with the experience of the Heideggerian mood; and since the wild experience in the park in December, and since falling deeply into myself (and not coming back) during the March session with David, these moods had been replaced with a mystical gift. In place of the moods, I was now being brought into the sacred and awesome presence of God during meditation.

I also realized that not only was I being brought into the presence of God, but that God had also been entering into me. I reflected on the sublime experiences I had in meditation: of Jesus entering into me, and me entering into Him; and of the flow I often felt of God moving in me and me moving in God.

In this heightened state of awareness, with great reverence, I considered that all this must constitute revelation. If something of the divine realm was being shown to me, then the word *revelation* was an accurate description. And, if so, then all along, without ever knowing it, I had been experiencing the revelation of God.

At last I knew that the *longing* I had experienced all of my life was in fact God's own longing for me. Joy.

The 'I AM' chants were continuing in meditation. One day the chant was:

I am in peace.
I am in love.
I am.

Once more, I received these sayings while appreciating the deeper meaning of the phrases when understood at the level of Being. I reflected on the two emphases that can be applied. On first reading, they can be descriptive of our state of mind, as a peaceful one, or a loving one. We might say, 'I am feeling peaceful' or, 'I am in a loving frame of mind.' These are descriptive statements *about* our state of being – states that can fluctuate and change moment to moment. This remains at the surface level.

But we can also appreciate them at a deeper level and lay the emphasis on our *beingness* in and of itself, so we understand that it is *only* in peace or *only* in love that we have our true being. When we place the emphasis this way, when we emphasize the 'I am' part of the sentence, then we can say, '*I am,* in love' which transforms it into a powerful statement of our 'beingness': '*I am,* in peace;' or, '*I am,* in love.' It becomes a statement of our higher being. I also realized that what was in play here was peace-itself and love-itself, as the true nature of God. Now I could say, '*I am,* in love,' or, '*I am,* in God,' as the purest statement of my being.

The third chant, the simple *I am* statement, gave me the most powerful learning of all. I realized that to be able to say, quite simply, 'I am' is the most profound statement of authentic being. When we no longer feel the egoic need to qualify our beingness with signifiers such as 'I am tall' or 'I am a lawyer' or even to state our name – 'I am Aedamar' – and we can move to simply saying 'I am', then we have entered our true being.

'I am' is the most powerful statement anyone could ever make – if it can be said without feeling that something is missing, or feeling as though there is a big void hanging at the end of the sentence. It can take a lifetime to dismantle all that we habitually add to our fundamental statement of being and identity. When we can simply say 'I am' without adding anything more, we know that we are whole.

I realized that it is only when we know we have our true being in love and in peace that we can really know our true selves – only then can we say, 'I am.' At last I was getting an inkling of what I might be able to contribute in seeking to build a career as a spiritual writer. I could help people to move into their authenticity and become comfortable simply saying 'I am.' And maybe I could help people to move from *I am* to *The I AM*. I began to understand that life is a crossing-over, a journey, from our small 'I am' to the glorious self-identifying claim of God in the Bible: 'I AM That I AM.' My small 'I am' has its whole being in The I AM and I find my true home when my little 'I am' comes home to rest in the Sacred Heart of The I AM. And there, I am, in the white light of Christ.

This move from I am to The I AM is the whole essence of the spiritual and mystical journey; this is the transformation of consciousness I discussed in the Introduction; this is the path to awakening I walk us through in Chapter 15 – the shift from knowing ourselves as I am to knowing ourselves as The I AM.

During another meditation the following exchange took place. I was inspired to say the first line: *I am in the white light of Christ.* Then God instantly replied, *I AM the White Light of Christ.* Fire! I finally figured out that these were essentially conversations with God, and also realized that God had been teaching me all along. I might say, 'I am peaceful,' then God would answer, 'I AM peace,' to illustrate how every last thing has its being in God. Whatever we are, or have of value, comes from God.

Slowly, very slowly, I was getting some ideas for what I could write as the spiritual writer I sensed I was to become.

By mid-September it was undeniable that I was entering what some writers call God-consciousness. I was omni-aware of the divine both in my beautiful meditations and in my new mystical perception of nature; and I was now slowly learning how to perceive the divine in people and in everyday life. I still did not understand that spiritual awakening is not 'a thing apart' in one's life, but that it effects the most radical shift in one's entire being and in one's whole life, so that nothing will ever be the same again. While I felt I was in the process of becoming who I am, moving from psychological authenticity into what I call my spiritual authenticity, I still had no idea how far-reaching this awakening was going to be for my future life.

On 15 September, which is my wedding anniversary, I had a most miraculous experience in meditation that went far beyond all that I had already experienced. It was through a guided meditation CD from Mike Booth of Aura-Soma called *The Ancient City*. Mike guides you to walk through an ancient city towards a temple, through two outer rooms, and then into an inner room where you meet 'someone'. The 'someone' I met was God.

As soon as the meditation began, my spirit was out of my body and I entered or became my light-self. I walked the guided journey as light and immediately felt the presence of an angel to my right taking the form of golden light. We entered the inner room of the temple together and Mike guided me to meet whomever was waiting for us. As soon as I entered, I perceived a phenomenal holy presence that I knew was God. I was filled with holy awe. The presence was formless, not even light, not even formless light; it was nothing and yet it was almost exploding with holy power. I knew with absolute certainty that I was in the presence of God. It was unbelievable. I was not burning but I was in deep, deep peace.

I was filled with staggering awe, knowing that what I perceived was the most sacred, holy and divine presence of the highest holiness.

As I stood in my light form in profound reverence before this awesome presence, instantly – quicker than the blink of an eye, quicker than a split second – I felt myself travel at the speed of light *into* the holy presence. I felt myself *become part* of the holy presence – barely noticing that I had been moved, it happened so fast. God absorbed me and made me one with Itself. I have no other way to explain what happened, except that I felt myself to have been absorbed into and become a part of that awesome presence that I knew was God. I felt *intense* peace.

When Mike's voice indicated it was time to leave the inner room of the temple, another miraculous thing happened. As I prepared to leave God – that is, to step back out of the presence of God and to walk away – God came with me without leaving Its own presence. And not just came to walk beside me as a presence, but God also kept me still within Itself as I walked, so that, as I later wrote in my diary, 'It was me-in-God that walked.'

Fire exploded inside my body: me-in-God. God walked for me. As if, when I walked, I was carried in God's holy presence. I did not walk alone. It was phenomenal, and completely inexplicable in human terms, but even more than that, in coming with me, God did not leave the place where I had been perceiving God as the central presence in the inner room. The presence of God remained unmoved, unchanged and undepleted, but nonetheless, God also came with me. God both moved and did not move.

It was staggering to experience: the wonder of God – without dividing, nonetheless coming with me – totally. I was full of God. Without dividing or separating from God-presence, God-and-I, as one, left the sacred presence of God. Yet, God did not diminish in any way by coming with me while equally fully remaining with Itself. It was a stunning paradox of God moving without moving, of dividing without dividing. Without dividing, God stayed, and yet came with me.

Mike's voice continued to guide me towards the end of the meditation, and to leave the temple. I felt myself to walk in this miraculous manner out of the temple and Mike's visualization guided me to be back out in the crowded marketplace. Once outside, and still in the meditation, I instantly saw that everyone else in the crowd was equally full of God and I had a new peaceful revelation of The I AM at the burning core of every being in existence. I cannot make it any clearer than this.

Words are completely inadequate to the task of describing what happened.

From this day on, my mystical experiences in meditation entered a new level of sacredness. It became the norm for me in my meditations to enter God or for God to enter me in the most profound manner imaginable, so that I knew myself as one-with-God, one-with-love, one-with-Christ, and belonging intimately somehow to Mary Magdalene. My understanding of the oneness of all, and in particular of my oneness with God, developed exponentially. I now strongly felt that I was 'being called', but I still did not know what I was being called to.

When I meditated on 19 September, I had another profound experience during the same *Ancient City* meditation. This time I experienced myself to merge with the presence of Christ and to become one with Him. I felt such a sense of belonging at the core of my being: Aedamar-Christ, One. As the meditation ended and I was guided by Mike to leave the inner temple, I had the experience of it being Christ who moved while holding me deep within Him, rather than my leaving on my own. I felt myself most sacredly to be *in* Jesus *in* The I AM. And I felt it was Jesus, The I AM, who carried me back out of the meditation. And I had an amazing new understanding that when I meet other people, I meet The I AM in them. I understood the glorious paradox of the undivided God manifesting in different beings. I felt intimately held by God. I thought to myself, *I no longer need to do anything on my own because it is God who acts through me.*

~

CHAPTER 10

INTELLECTUAL VISION

*'This is called an intellectual vision;
I cannot tell why.'*
ST TERESA OF ÁVILA

As the year wore on, I was becoming a little bit more confident at navigating my way along this extraordinary spiritual path, and I was also very curious. It was hard to believe how much had happened in the 10 months since David had first suggested meditation to me. David had also introduced me to Eileen Elizabeth Heneghan, the therapist and Seichim Reiki master, and in October she invited me to join a Reiki Level 1 Initiation. If the invitation had been offered just a year beforehand, I would have been far too nervous to explore Reiki, but by this point I knew I was protected by the white light of Christ and that it was safe to explore further. Eileen is a wise and holy woman and I also knew I would be safe in her care.

The Reiki Initiation took place over a beautiful autumnal weekend in October. We all stayed in Clonacody, an elegant Georgian guesthouse set on gorgeous grounds in Tipperary – it was a real treat of a weekend. Eileen holds a profoundly sacred space for people. The initiation was powerful and holy, but I will not describe it here. Eileen also led us in several guided meditations. During one of the meditations, a beautiful exchange took place between God and me. In my mind I heard myself spontaneously speaking a short phrase and then I heard God reply, using almost the same words but transforming them utterly with the power of The I AM:

I am healing
I AM Healing.

I am alive
I AM Life.

I am alight
I AM Light.

I am in the Light
I AM the Light.

I am in peace
I AM Peace.

I am in Love
I AM Love.

I am
I AM.

I came both to understand and to feel how closely related we are to the divine. All that we can ever say of ourselves is made possible by the divine I AM. In the English language we even use the same words to describe ourselves: I am, I AM. Where does the difference truly lie? I realized it can be a sacred thing to say 'I am' and to recognize our intimate belonging to The I AM Itself.

As the weekend ended I felt alight and alive in love. I was feeling more attuned to and understanding of the mystical gift I was receiving, and I knew myself to be blessed. All the same, I was still remarkably naive. I still thought that I needed the gift of 'vision' or 'the sight', to complete the picture. I thought that would be *proof* that the divine was genuinely communicating with me.

As I drove home to Dublin from Tipperary, I was asking God for the gift of 'vision'. Next thing, I heard myself speaking spontaneously in my head. Crystal clear, quite sharply and with a strong tone of irritation in my voice, I heard myself say, *I did get vision. I got intellectual vision.* I could not believe my ears, and I knew by the tone of exasperation that I was being chastised about my irritating demands for more than I was already receiving. Yet, when I 'spoke' those words, holy fire ran through my body. I had never heard the phrase 'intellectual vision' before and I did not understand what it meant, but it came with the stamp of truth and I knew it was divinely inspired.

I had, however, heard of 'intellectual intuition'. In philosophy, we had learned about the three levels of knowing, also called intuition: sensible intuition; rational intuition; and intellectual intuition. At the first level of sensible intuition, we know something through the senses – by touch, taste, sight, smell or hearing. At the second level, we know by the use of our reasoning mind. At the third level, we know something intuitively, without the use of reason – we simply intuit something to be true by the power of the mind. Such an intuition is unprovable but carries within it the stamp of its own truth – it proves itself to be true. A good example of this type of intuition is Descartes' statement: 'I think, therefore I am.' He said it came to him 'clear and distinct', not through rational analysis.

When I heard those words, *I did get vision, I got intellectual vision*, I felt it as a truth, although I did not understand what it meant. The tone of voice, even though it was my own voice speaking in my head, was akin to an irritated parent correcting a child for the umpteenth time. I dropped the topic.

Approximately one year later, when reading a book by the highly regarded scholar of mysticism Evelyn Underhill, called *Mysticism: A Study in the Nature and Development of Spiritual Consciousness*, I came upon the term 'intellectual vision'. I had all but forgotten that previous exchange, but now it came back to me forcefully, powerfully, as I read that the term refers to the highest of the three levels of mystical vision available. The other two are imaginary vision and corporeal vision. In describing intellectual vision as 'closely connected with the consciousness of the Presence of God', Underhill draws primarily on the visions and writings of two female Christian mystics, Angela of Foligno, of the 13th century, and St Teresa of Ávila, of the 16th century, both of whom separately but similarly describe a type of vision that is completely formless. Underhill says that intellectual vision:

> [Seems] to be a something not sought but put before the mind and seen or perceived by the whole self by means of a sense which is neither sight nor feeling but partakes of the character of both. It is intimate but indescribable: definite yet impossible to define.

St Angela described it as follows:

> At times God comes into the soul without being called; and He instils into her fire, love, and sometimes sweetness; and the soul believes this comes from God and delights therein... This feeling of God gives her the greatest delight... And beyond this the soul receives the gift of seeing God. God says to her, 'Behold Me!' and the soul sees Him dwelling within her... And the soul rejoices in that sight with an ineffable joy; and this is the manifest and certain sign that God indeed dwells in her.

St Teresa later introduced the term 'intellectual vision' to describe exactly that highest state of vision that 'carries more conviction than bodily sight' and that can last for several days or even, in her case, for over a year. In this type of vision, St Teresa wrote that she was conscious that Jesus Christ was standing by her side, although she did not perceive Him with the eyes of the body or of the soul. She wrote, 'This is called an intellectual vision; I cannot tell why.'

St Teresa also described how 'such a vision brings with it a special knowledge of God, and a most tender love for God results from being constantly in God's company and that the desire to devote one's whole being to the service of God is more fervent than ever before.'

I was shocked and stunned. She was describing precisely my own sacred experiences.

Of all the shocks I had received along the road in this spiritual journey, this was the most serious. I felt chastened and ashamed. I felt that up until that moment, I had been playing games with the glorious gift I had been receiving. Here, in black and white, I was learning that I had been receiving the greatest possible revelation of the divine without ever knowing it. Even as I write these words, over a year later, my head is on fire remembering how humbled I felt to discover how unspeakably blessed I actually was. I vividly remember the exact moment I read those passages. I was sitting reading at our dining table and supervising my son, who was doing his homework at the far end. I recall the shock going through me as a bolt of lightning.

This changed my attitude entirely. I began to take everything a lot more seriously. I stopped my immature demands for proof from God that it was in fact God I was meeting in heaven in my meditations. I stopped questioning the miracle of the leaves and the roses in my garden. I had every reason to be ashamed of my delay in responding appropriately to God, who had blessed me in this staggering way.

~

CHAPTER 11

AT THE DEFINING CROSSROADS OF MY LIFE

'Two roads diverged in a wood, and I –
I took the one less travelled by,
And that has made all the difference.'
ROBERT FROST, FROM 'THE ROAD NOT TAKEN'

At this point my narrative returns to the events of October 2015, when I was once more facing a great sadness in my life. My mother was not long for this world, and so I stood yet again at that sacred place of transition where I had stood with my father only a year previously. I have no doubt that these experiences of grief and loss heightened my sensitivity to, and awareness of, the spiritual realm. My mind turned further inwards as I contemplated the experience of life, love and death.

In the days just before my mother passed through to the other realm, a new visionary element and a deeper level of stillness opened up to me in meditation, which then established itself as a consistent pattern. It may have been influenced by my repeated readings for my mother of St John of the Cross' mystical poem *Dark Night of the Soul*, with its wondrous imagery of climbing a secret ladder to God in contemplation:

> *'In darkness and secure*
> *By secret ladder disguised, Oh happy chance!'*

One morning, as I began to meditate, in my mind's eye I saw myself begin to climb a dusty old stone spiral staircase, such as you would see in any small medieval church in Europe. It became more of a vision than a meditation, and as I climbed, unable to see beyond the next two or three steps of the spiral, I asked myself where this staircase might lead. Quickly I came to understand that it was an exercise in trust in going into the unknown. I was to climb, without knowing where I was going. And in fact, the stairs ultimately led nowhere. At the top, they simply left the building and opened out into pitch-black night sky.

I knew that I was being asked to trust myself to step off into 'the nothing' without fearing that I would fall. The vision was so real that if I had imagined myself falling, I knew I would feel my body fall. I willed myself to become absolutely still, and felt myself to become pure nothing, so that it did not matter whether I had solid ground beneath me or not. I became utterly still, and I trusted. Then, in the vision, I stepped off the edge and I did not fall. I held myself up by my pure belief and trust. Having stepped into the nothing, I said to God, *I am here*. Instantly God replied, *I AM Here*. Fire exploded in my head.

At that point, the garb I had been wearing in the vision – a brown-grey dress, as if I were a medieval nun – changed into a white cloak with a rainbow of chakra colours shining down my front. In seeing my clothing transforming, I felt like I were stepping into my true spiritual self. I was on fire. Then I saw a powerful, blazing light in front of me and I knew it was God.

Afterwards, I knew that it had been a lesson in *stillness*. I understood the need for absolute stillness and deep silence in order for God to have any chance of shining in us. God will not compete with the noise of the world. I understood that we need to reach this level of stillness, of being nothing-in-the-nothing, in order to be with God. God said to me, *You find me in the stillness, because I AM the Stillness.*

After my mother's death, in the liminal space of my grief, I seriously began to consider what was required of me in return for the gift I was receiving – what could I do to repay God? I reflected often on the incredibly direct guidance I was given on the beach in Mayo: *Give back what you have received by describing it.*

My firm conviction was that I could not share the visions themselves because nobody would believe me. Above all, I did not want to say I was a mystic. I thought I would be regarded as a lunatic. I feared I would lose all credibility among my friends and peers and that it would compromise the chance of getting the novel I was writing published. There were so many reasons to write *around* the experiences rather than to admit to them *directly*. I wondered if I could tell the story of my spiritual awakening without saying anything about the mystical experiences. This, of course, would prove impossible.

As the months wore on, I was engrossed in writing my novel, *Hollow Street*. It was a comfort and a pleasure to be absorbed in the creative process. The protagonist of *Hollow Street*, Eala Ealú, (which is Irish for 'the lost swan') had suffered psychological trauma in utero, was born with a fractured psyche and could not relate to the world as others did. Living homeless, in a liminal space between sanity and insanity, she was unable to understand herself or to be understood by others. She lived with a desperate and seemingly incoherent longing 'to have birth', as she called it.

Eala became entirely real to me and I learned to surrender to the story she was living through, rather than making it up myself. I learned to act more as a diviner, intuiting her story, feeling it, sensing it, calling it in, channelling it and almost letting it write itself onto the pages of the book. I followed her traumatized psyche to the edge of language, to the edge of meaning and to the edge of sanity, exploring her frustrated efforts to understand and be understood. I accepted the challenge, on her behalf, to express the inexpressible, describe the indescribable, say the unsayable and speak the unspeakable.

I soon saw the keen similarities between the creative and the spiritual processes. The patterns were almost identical; for example: surrender; trust; intuition; and reading energies. I was developing the confidence to write my novel as it wanted to be written, throwing out the literary rules and traditions, admittedly to the concern of our professor of creative writing. I trusted myself to write a radically postmodern novel about a lost and misunderstood soul, searching for mother love, and this helped me to trust more in the mystical gift that was developing at exactly the same time. Inevitably, Eala developed her own mystical gift, and equally inevitably, it was not understood by those around her. Instead she was committed to long-term care in a psychiatric hospital.

By the time I finished writing my novel, in the spring of 2017, I knew I stood at the defining crossroads of my life. Would I proceed with my plans to become a novelist, try to get my novel published and begin exciting PhD studies, or would I respond to this close-to-unfathomable 'call' by giving up these hard-won opportunities and try to find my way on the spiritual path?

Somehow, there was no choice.

Even though I could not see the way forwards, and could not imagine how to earn a living as a spiritual writer, and was unsure of what I could even write about in a spiritual book; and even though I was confused and sad to be abandoning my passion for academia and forfeiting my career as a novelist; and even though I was scared of the social implications for me and my family, and worried for the ridicule my children would face; and even though I faced strong resistance to it all from my husband; and even though I was vacillating wildly between courage and hopelessness, and had absolutely nobody to help me – *somehow, there was no choice.*

The deepest sense, which I now carried inside me, was silent wonder and awe at the incredible holiness of life – not just my own life, but also life itself... *and somehow, there was no choice.*

But it was one thing to decide to 'go public' with the message of love, and another thing entirely to know how to go about doing so. I had no way of situating my experiences within a known context. I did not know anything sensible about awakening itself. I had got to the age of 46 without ever encountering the language, the context or the understanding needed to meet this spiritual, and then mystical, awakening with any degree of understanding. There was nothing in my Catholic upbringing, my education by Catholic nuns or in the entirety of my Catholic Church that had ever given me – or anyone around me – any insight at all into the lived experience of spiritual awakening.

> *I still did not properly understand that*
> *I was undergoing a spiritual awakening*
> *as a recognizable life event.*

I was doing my best to process the experiences within the privacy of my mind and private life, and even though the last thing in the world I wanted to do was admit to these mystical experiences publicly, that was what I was nonetheless committed to doing.

There was no context in the entire landscape of my life into which my experiences fitted in any meaningful and straightforward way. This ought to have rendered them meaningless. But they were not meaningless. They were profound, beautiful and deeply and intrinsically meaningful in and of themselves. That had to mean there was something fundamental missing in my life context, and in my religion in particular, that failed to explain or accommodate them in any meaningful way for me. Where was the expertise that could, and maybe should, have helped me to understand and process all that was happening to me?

I was still scared to speak of it with my husband, my family or my friends. I knew they would struggle to believe me, and would most likely think I had become a religious freak or a crazy woman. When I finally did, tentatively, tell my husband something of what was happening, he said to me, not all that lovingly, 'Aedamar, only crazy people say that Jesus talks to them.' The two friends I reached out to both recoiled.

Over a year into this turmoil, I slowly began to tell David, my craniosacral therapist, a tiny bit about what was happening. I was still hesitant and frightened, and thought it was far beyond the remit of what I could reasonably expect him to help me with, but I had a deep human need to be heard. I just touched on the surface of what was happening, but it was a relief to say anything at all to someone who listened. Later on, when it became clear it was safe to trust him with the holiest of my experiences, sacred events often unfolded during my sessions, so that he was witness to conversations with Jesus and a life-changing visitation by Mary Magdalene. The day Mary Magdalene came to me, she poured a river of fire into me through the crown of my head and said it would not stop until I accepted that I embody the energy of Mary Magdalene. In awe and deep humility, I accepted. Then she said to me, as she has said many other times: 'Speak for me as I was not allowed to speak.'

In the end, I turned in desperation to my sometime-church. It took huge courage to speak aloud about what was going on, but unfortunately they were not interested and refused to help me in any way. On three separate occasions they turned me away, treating me like the kind of lunatic they think gives religion a bad name.

My first approach was to a Discalced Carmelite priest and academic theologian from the Pontifical Theological Faculty, *Teresianum*, in Rome. He was visiting Dublin to lead the 2016 Christmas celebrations in the church of St Teresa of Ávila. On Christmas Day, he gave a powerfully moving, mystically exhilarating sermon on the opening lines of the Gospel of John: 'In the beginning was the Word, and the Word was with God, and the Word was God.' I was deeply touched and on fire spiritually. I thought here at last was someone who would be receptive to my story.

After Mass I asked to meet with him privately. We met the next day and he listened with respect but also with fear. He was clearly uncomfortable with what I was saying. When I finished, he said he was out of his depth with what I was sharing and he could not help. Ironically, his Discalced Carmelite order follows the tradition of St Teresa of Ávila and St John of the Cross –

two of Christianity's greatest mystics – so if he was out of his depth, where did that leave me? He ended with this sentence: 'If God wants your story to be told, it will be told.' It was unclear whether this was meant to encourage or to discourage me.

The next effort I made to get some help and guidance was to attend a retreat in the Jesuit retreat house, Manresa, in North Dublin. In order to speak privately with the priest in charge of the retreat I had to be 'vetted' by a nun, meaning that I had to tell her what I wanted to talk to the priest about. In that little exchange the nun was disrespectful and ridiculed me, suggesting it was fanciful for me to be saying the things I was saying. Defensively, I retorted, 'I am completely psychologically stable.' To which she rudely and derisively replied, 'How do you know that?' I was deeply upset.

She did allow me to proceed to the priest who, when I nervously shared with him my holy experiences, effectively dismissed me as he would a child with a far-fetched story and as good as patted me on the head. He said, 'Don't be troubling yourself about things like that.' I was devastated and angry. My own church, disinterested, turning me away, refusing to help. I had not expected this response.

Nonetheless, I still longed for some guidance or support, so I signed up with a spiritual director for paid private sessions. Her training was with the Jesuits and unfortunately, the story yet again was of more fear, more rules, more 'don't go there' – not quite calling me crazy woman, but extremely wary. She was kind and respectful but very fearful. She did not like what I was sharing one little bit. She reminded me, many times, that just because someone has visions of the light, they do not necessarily come from the light, that the devil can masquerade as light. It was St John of the Cross all over again.

My frustration was intense and, when I cried in despair at her attitude, she suggested I was crying because I was not comfortable to be having what she referred to as 'these so-called visions'. I was crying because she was trying to fit me into the ABC of her non-mystical training manual, and I could not fit. When I told her that I sometimes had inner visions of Jesus at Mass, she said, 'Ignore all that and focus on the priest.' It was clear to me that she had absolutely no concept of what it is like to receive a vision of Jesus – there is no option to ignore it. I gave up the sessions.

My final attempt to get some help was to approach one of my philosophy professors, whom I could discern had his own mystical gift. He kindly but firmly resisted my effort to engage his assistance, although he did give me two books on the philosophy of mysticism that were on the bookshelf in his office.

By now, I felt utterly hopeless and abandoned by life. Why would nobody help me? I wondered, was I a fool? Was I making an idiot of myself? After all, this was the 21st century – things like this did not even happen anymore. People did not get 'called', or have visions or mystical experiences. Plus, it was too late to become a nun. Maybe I had it all wrong. Maybe I should try to forget everything that was happening to me, try to get on with my life, stick with my original plans and try to get my novel published. But I could not. The depth and the beauty of all that I was experiencing in meditation was so powerful and compelling that, even if no one would help me, I knew I had to find a way forwards on my own. And that was exactly where I now stood – completely and utterly on my own.

PART II

~

REPLACING THE NARRATIVE OF SEPARATION WITH A NARRATIVE OF LOVE

The real poor are the rich.
The real hungry are the overfed.
No one is truly rich until they can give
away all they do not need.

My words are jewels.
I have filled your treasure chest; share them with the world.
Spread my jewels before their feet
And lay a Pathway before them
That leads them home to Love.

My children hunger for my Word.
Share all that I have shared with you.
Give back to me by giving to them in my holy name.

Feed the poor of spirit,
Feed the poor of heart,
Feed the poor of mind,
Feed the poor of the world
With my holy food.

The real poor are not the homeless lying on the
side of the road with hunger in their bellies.
The real poor are the rich.
The real hungry are the overfed.
Their hunger is not of this world.
Their hunger is eternal hunger – hunger for things
they don't even know that they need.
Their hunger is for God, and they don't even know it.

Share my jewels with the truly hungry.
Lay before them a Path of Gold enlightened with my Love.

JESUS

CHAPTER 12

WAKING UP TO DIVINE LOVE

'I AM not, without you.'
VOICE OF GOD

Waking up to love was the most beautiful event of my life, but it also caused me to feel deep personal pain about the state that humanity is in. I became radically sensitive to suffering and disharmony of all forms, both at home and in the wider world. How could I reconcile my absolute knowing that all is one in God, with our universally lived experience of pain, brokenness, turmoil and dis-ease?

Whereas, before my awakening, I had lazily presumed that governments, the UN, aid agencies and charities were responsible for fixing these world problems, now it became crystal clear that *each one of us* is responsible. It was no longer an option to sit back and hope that someone else would act. I felt a strong sense of calling to do something myself. But, if I was to find a way to contribute to healing the world through my writing, I needed to understand what had set humanity on its insane spiral of self-destruction. What causes us to be living these spiritually bereft, broken and traumatized lives? And why do we desecrate and destroy our home on Mother Earth?

It soon became clear to me that at the heart of our brokenness there lies a mistaken belief in a fundamental separation between humanity and God – a separation that does not in fact exist. We have misunderstood the nature of God; we have misunderstood our own nature; and we have misunderstood the nature of our relationship to God – all of which, in turn, causes us to misunderstand the meaning and purpose of life.

I wanted to find out where, when and how this belief in separation entered our thinking, and what had caused it to gain such a stranglehold on Western consciousness, when everything of my mystical experiences showed me that it was not true.

It became the work of my soul to figure out why we do not live at the level of beauty, truth and love, but have chosen instead pain, brokenness and trauma.

My enquiries quickly led me back to the historical period known as the 'Axial Age', which spanned 800–200BCE. The philosopher Karl Jaspers coined the term Axial Age to describe this period of profound and evolutionary shift for humanity – the time when reasoning and intellectual thought first emerged. Most people do not realize just how young our capacity to reason actually is. The Axial Age was also the beginning of the 'modern' human era that we are living in today.

THE BIRTH OF REASON

This spontaneous eruption of intellectual thought occurred in diverse pockets all across the world: in ancient Greece – Socrates, Plato, Aristotle; in China – Confucius; in India – Buddha; in the Middle East – the Hebrew Prophets; and many more. Philosophers call it the Golden Age, when intellectual thought became an activity in its own right. It marked the time when philosophers began to answer their questions about life without recourse to mythology or to supernatural explanations attributable to the gods. Instead they began to look within, to the power of their own intellectual reasoning, to answer the questions of life.

Back then, as now, the ancients were engaged with the 'big questions', in particular the most important question of all: what is the nature of the relationship between humanity and God? This is a religious question, but in the Axial Age it acquired a philosophical expression in the question known as: 'the one and the many'. Both of these questions are asking the same thing: how do the parts belong to the whole? They point to the human impulse to seek unity in diversity, wholeness in multiplicity, similarity in difference and belonging in division.

These questions address the paradox that, while we perceive ourselves as separate, individual human beings, living separate, individual lives, surrounded by multiplicity and diversity, we nonetheless intuit order behind the chaos. We instinctively sense that there is a higher, intelligent, organizing principle behind all that we see, which explains the belonging together of multiplicity in a meaningful whole. Religions call this organizing principle 'God' and the God of religion is deemed to be either being, intelligence or love, or all three. Philosophy calls it the 'Logos', which is the universal pattern of all things. Science then joined the search, looking for the scientific principle that will explain how all of nature hangs together in a meaningful whole, but to date it has not been found.

Prior to the Axial Age, and the birth of reason, humanity lived in profound, symbiotic relationship with nature and the spirit of life. All of life was unquestionably deemed to be innately spiritual. Animism is the term used to describe the belief that nature and life are profoundly suffused with spirit. The ancients unquestionably believed that life was spiritual. They already intuited the Earth to be the living organism that it is. Life was known to be sacred, and nature known to be 'enchanted'. The existence of higher powers and ordering principles of life, in the form of goddesses and gods, was taken for granted – not as a primitive misunderstanding of things, but as a profound inner knowing that this was true.

For tens of millennia prior to reasoning, humanity already had many rich and diverse meaning-making systems that were used to make sense of the world and our presence in it. Just think of the 35,000-year-old cave paintings. These meaning-making practices included myth, magic, poetry, story, song, dance, art, intuition, ritual, initiation, spirituality, religion, sacred practices and worship of nature. These were, and remain, incredibly rich and fertile meaning-making systems in their own right.

THE PRIVILEGING OF REASON ABOVE SPIRIT

With the birth of reason, everything changed, especially the manner in which this central question, of how the parts belong to the whole, was answered. Reason was obviously game-changing for humanity. The incredible gifts and benefits it has given to us are undeniable and need no elaboration. Almost immediately, however, a major problem unfolded in the way reason was employed and deployed in the West, because the newly rational ancients wrongly believed that reason had come to replace, rather than to complement, all that had gone before it. Instead of integrating reason with all pre-existing wisdom systems, especially our spiritual wisdom, reason became the dominant and near-exclusive tool for understanding ourselves, the world and our presence in it. The guiding intuition of an underlying, unifying principle weakened, because our intuition itself weakened.

The 'rational animal', as Aristotle termed the new human in around 320BCE, fancied itself as sophisticated and advanced; no longer in thrall to what was thought of as a witch's brew of meaning-making practices, of the myth and magic that had served humanity for millennia. Instead of building on the wisdom of the ancients, and integrating it with the new faculty of reason, the now rational philosophers and thinkers elevated reason above all other forms of meaning-making. They privileged and prioritized reason, regarding the old practices as primitive, outdated and unsuited to the now rationalized world. They came to believe that reason alone could answer life's problems and complexities.

Increasingly, attention was on the parts rather than the whole; on the many instead of the one. We found ourselves more and more lost in a world of multiplicity, diversity, division and separation; increasingly alienated from God, nature, each other and ourselves. Our relationship with the whole began to fracture.

THE DE-SPIRITUALIZATION OF THE WORLD

In privileging reason over the wisdom of spirit and the traditions of myth, story, intuition, ritual and religion, among others, the rational thinkers performed what was later called the 'disenchantment and the de-spiritualization of the world'. It was the philosophers Theodor Adorno and Max Horkheimer who introduced this revelatory perspective and explication of how reason came to dominate our culture and civilization. These two German Jewish philosophers, living in exile during World War II in New York, set up a branch of The Frankfurt School of Critical Theory at Columbia University. They were determined to identify the roots of the barbarism that led to World War II. They knew that dominant culture is always built on an underlying philosophy. Therefore, Enlightenment culture and thinking – the dominant ideology of the West – was also necessarily built on an underlying philosophy. Their goal was to identify that underlying philosophy and name it as the root cause of World War II.

In their famous book *Dialectic of Enlightenment*, they located the foundational philosophy of modern Enlightenment culture, and therefore the war that came out of it, all the way back in the

Axial Age. They saw that it was as early as the time of Plato and Aristotle that a foundational *rational* philosophy had been adopted by Western culture. It was back then that reason was elevated above all other forms of wisdom and the project of disenchantment, demythologizing and 'de-spiritualizing' the world first began. (Remember, it was Plato who banished the poets from the ideal republic.) Adorno and Horkheimer identified this era as the time in which the sacred was lost from everyday life; when we lost our innate understanding of the spirituality of life and of nature; and when we lost our sense of connection to the whole. Their work is a scathing analysis of the history of Western culture and civilization that led to war, and to the neo-barbaric consumerist culture of greed and selfishness we live with today. Spirituality had been airbrushed out of life and history because reason thought it could go it alone.

THE LOSS OF WONDER AND AWE

An inevitable consequence of losing the sacred from life was that with it went our sense of wonder and awe before all of creation. Wonder and awe express our natural fascination before the magnificence of life. To suppress, repress and oppress any natural impulse results in that energy being expressed in a deformed or pathological manner. We know from psychology that, when our emotions and impulses are not expressed in a healthy, straightforward manner, they will be expressed in substitutionary symptomology or pathology – such as addiction, self-harm, depression and low self-esteem, for example.

The same thing has happened through our blocking of our innate ability to feel and express our natural spirituality and our natural connection to the whole. By living through the lens of reason we block our instinctive wonder and awe before nature, before life and before God, and instead it comes out in distorted ways. The symptomology and pathology of our Western greed for ever more material goods and wealth is a perverted expression of our natural desire to feel a sense of awe during the ordinary course of life. People amass money, designer lives and other expressions of ego-satisfaction in a deluded effort to respond to our natural impulse to be awed by life.

Capitalism explicitly manipulates our desire for awe and for 'more' by giving us a temporary 'retail rush'; by selling a disposable life that needs constant renewing and replenishing. People chase after money, power and prestige in a vain attempt to experience something resembling our lost sense of awe. The 'more' that people seek is, in fact, the 'more' that entirely transcends material goods, namely the spiritual. But capitalism manipulates this desire for 'more' and subtly engenders in us a mindset of 'need' for the material things of our phony Photoshopped culture of greed. Everybody knows that, in its current iteration, capitalism serves to make the rich richer and the poor poorer.

The success of capitalism explicitly depends on consumers *not* waking up. If we knew how to stand before the sheer miracle of existence in awe, if our spirituality was properly developed and integrated, we would not care about locations, labels, titles and wealth.

Tragically, therefore, it was in the earliest expression of our intellectual brilliance that respect for God, nature and humanity was lost from life. Reason wanted to go it alone, instead of realizing that it was – an admittedly magnificent – part of a magnificent whole.

Dualism and the Binary Mind

While still acknowledging the brilliance of reason, we cannot deny that another of its central features – dualistic, 'either/or' thinking – unfortunately contributed further to the fracturing of our relationship with the whole. The brilliance of this central characteristic of reason is that it helps to place order on things – it separates, divides, categorizes and sorts things, each under its own separate heading. This organizing principle was ground-breaking in terms of establishing order on the world: things that are alike are placed together, and things that are not alike are separated and kept apart.

While this revolutionary contribution of reason was invaluable, it was precisely in privileging this impulse to separate and divide that the dualistic, binary attitude was allowed to dominate and shape modern Western thinking. Without the leavening agent of spirit and a commitment to the whole, reason stamped the primacy of dualism and binary thought into the heart of Enlightenment thinking and civilization.

A consciousness based on separation and division inevitably leads to rupture, and this is the rupture that lies at the heart of our broken civilization today: rupture between reason and spirit; spirit and matter; humanity and nature, and the other ruptures that I outlined in the Introduction. These are the wounds that disfigure the landscape of our life and culture today. They are the pathologies of a naive and unwise infatuation with reason and all that it could do.

REINTRODUCING THE SACRED BACK INTO LIFE

No one is calling for a return to primitive pre-rational times. But what we are calling for is a recognition that the pre-rational wisdom practices were not primitive. They were in fact highly sophisticated, spiritually engaged, rich meaning-making systems that we now desperately need to recover. It is crucial to appreciate the scale of the mistake we have made in thinking that life could be run on the track of reason alone.

We urgently need to reintroduce the sacred back into life; to re-embrace it as an integral element for understanding ourselves and the world in which we live. We need to recover our natural sense of awe, wonder, curiosity and respect, and to heal the rifts between reason and spirit; spirit and matter; humanity and nature; masculine and feminine; between each other, and also within our own selves.

When we lost our non-rational practices, we lost the ability fully to understand ourselves and the meaning of life in a holistic way. Our anthropocentric arrogance makes us think that we dictate to life which parts we will take and which parts we will reject.

But, just as in times past, when we had to accept that the sun does not revolve around the Earth and that the Earth is not flat, now we must accept that the rational mind is not the centre point around which life and the galaxy spins. Instead, it is a small part of a magnificent whole that has unfortunately been mistaken *for the whole*. Our spirituality is not an optional extra, but integral and life-critical to who we are, how we function properly and how we understand ourselves and life.

We urgently need to restore our spirituality alongside our rationality, and to develop mature spiritual consciousness, if we are to have any hope of saving our species and our beautiful planet.

Richard Kearney, the brilliant Irish philosopher at Boston College, Massachusetts, shared a wonderful idea in a talk he gave in Dublin. He spoke of 'theism' as an immature spirituality – a simple enough unquestioning belief in God. This is inevitably followed by 'atheism' – a rejection of that God because our maturing mind questions, and our spirit seeks experience that cannot be provided at that level. Atheism, however, is properly followed by 'anatheism', which is a return to God in order to be in a mature, sophisticated relationship with the divine, as equals, one with one.

Our culture, as a secular society, is in atheism. We have rejected God and spirituality, but we ought not stay there. We ought to grow up and mature, and come back to God again in a new way, seeking a mature spiritual-mystical relationship with God –

knowing ourselves as belonging most profoundly, as light in the light, and as love in love.

The time is now, urgently, to re-embrace the sacred. We are sleepwalking through life, unaware that our failure to awaken is the cause of the brokenness of our culture and civilization today. Life is a gift that, tragically, we do not understand. As a species, we have lost our way.

Let's you and me now try to find it again.

~

CHAPTER 13

CHILDREN OF THE LIGHT

'Believe in the light, then, while you have it,
so that you will be the people of the light.'
JESUS, GOSPEL OF JOHN

There was a further historic mis-step that compounded and aggravated the mindset of division and rupture that was developing in the emerging modern Western psyche. It is found most unexpectedly in Christianity – in the narrative of separation used to explain our relationship with God, and also in Christianity's emphasis on doctrinal theology over spiritual care of the soul, both of which contributed further to our sense of alienation from God.

Just 200 years into the new Age of Reason, a mere second in the overall timeline of humanity, Jesus came into the world as the human incarnation of divine love. He came with a radical message of love, with the message that we are children of the light, and that the whole purpose and point of life is to wake up to the light that we already are. His presence, his essence, his teachings, his whole life and death, were a singular expression and embodiment of divine love. Jesus followed no law other than his own inner law of love. He lived his message of love, peace, harmony, justice, equality, gender equality, care for the poor, the sick, the lonely, the persecuted and also for the natural world. His message, then as now, was a perfect correction to our belief in separation, and to the aberrant use of our highest faculty.

So, what went wrong?

Here I offer a sketch of six key events in Christian history that lie at the heart of what has gone wrong for Christianity, Christians and Christian culture. These are:

— The narrative of separation enshrined in the Story of Eve and Adam;

— The adoption of Christianity as the official religion of the Roman Empire;

— The Hellenization of Christianity;

— St Augustine's doctrine of original sin;

— The rejection of meditation and mysticism as central religious practices for all;

— The codification of the canonical Bible that rejected all female writing.

Acknowledging, before I begin, all the beauty and the good contributed by Christianity, including religious worship, art, music, architecture, education, their care for the poor, the sick, the uneducated and the dispossessed; and acknowledging also the pain, suffering and trauma inflicted elsewhere by Christianity, and by Catholicism in particular, it is not my purpose to address these elements in any way. I acknowledge also that, since the Council of Vatican II in 1968, Christianity has softened the domineering attitude of power and control it had hitherto displayed in defining itself as the one true religion. Since then, it has moved towards a better understanding of the love of Jesus for all, and the role of all religions in contributing to the search for God, but once again, it is not my purpose to address these perspectives in any way. My focus is on finding out why Christianity does not, and never did, assume responsibility for supporting the mature development of embodied spiritual-mystical consciousness for its lay followers, and often for its religious members, too.

THE NARRATIVE OF SEPARATION

Central to Christian teaching and theology, but contrary to the teaching of Jesus, is the flawed idea that there is a fundamental separation between God and humanity. We find it in the first book of the Bible, the Book of Genesis, which contains the Judeo–Christian creation myth, and the story of the 'fall'. The 'fall' is the fall of humanity out of oneness with God due to the sinning of Eve and Adam. The authors of Genesis, presumed to be writing in around the 6th or 5th century BCE, were trying to understand and explain – in myth, which was the method appropriate to their time – the nature of the relationship between humanity and God. They were trying to explain our seeming separation from the whole.

They concluded that we must once have belonged in perfection with God, but through some fault on our part we were exiled from this state of perfection and punished with finite human life on Earth. Essentially, they thought we had been able to undo God's plan for our species: that God had made us perfect, and that somehow we had undone God's work, and for this we were 'punished' with life on this extraordinarily beautiful planet. That was the thinking – that finitude and life on Earth were deserved punishments and self-induced disasters.

It does not matter that Genesis was a myth. The mythical nature of the narrative is irrelevant – what is relevant is that this mythological telling of our origin and creation reflects and perpetuates their belief in a foundational, fundamental and fatal separation between humanity and God. First through Judaism, and then Christianity, this belief was inscribed into the psyche and soul of the emerging modern Western human being. The newly rational mindset of division was now further compounded by this narrative of separation, of being lost and of resolute finitude.

Thus, at the heart of Christianity lies the fatal dualism of a split between humanity and God.

Five critical things then happened for Christianity, between the 4th and 5th centuries, that dramatically altered the course of its unfolding, and consequently the unfolding of Western consciousness and civilization itself.

THE ADOPTION OF CHRISTIANITY BY THE ROMAN EMPIRE

The death knell of Christianity as a Christ-centric, person-focused, mystically alive religion of love was sounded almost in its earliest iteration, when it was adopted as the official religion of the Roman Empire by Constantine in the 4th century. Constantine was the first emperor to convert to Christianity. By giving his official recognition to Christianity, which up to then had been a fringe and illegal religion, the Christian faith grew hand in hand with the most powerful political force of the day. While this was, of course, a great validation of Christianity, and could have created an unparalleled opportunity to spread Jesus' message of love, instead it led to his beautiful teachings becoming secondary to the desire to build the Church up into a power structure commensurate with the Roman Empire.

Such was the power and control the Christian Church came to wield in Europe that its teachings and culture became synonymous with Western culture and civilization for 2,000 years.

Christianity adopted the Roman Empire model of top-down, hierarchical, centralized, patriarchal power over the people – especially over women. And what was worse, they adopted a 'Roman Emperor' model in relation to God, making their masculine God a transcendent, distant, omnipotent, all-controlling, angry being, separate and unrelatable to ordinary people living ordinary, and often very difficult, lives.

Instead of guiding people to the light through love, as Jesus had done, by supporting mature spiritual growth in small mystical communities, the focus instead was on building up the institutional Church into a power structure. Despite the fact that Jesus had eschewed traditional expressions of power in favour of humble servant-leadership, the Church that established itself in his name succumbed to the very power structures and practices that Jesus had rejected to the death.

THE HELLENIZATION OF CHRISTIANITY

Equally, Jesus eschewed intellectual teaching in favour of stories, parables and miracles to share his transformative and healing message of love. Once it was free to do so, however, the Church quickly embraced the dominant intellectual teachings of the Roman Empire – specifically Greek philosophy – and performed what is known as the Hellenization of Christianity. This refers to the explicit adoption of Greek (Hellenic) intellectual ideas in order to give the new religion a strong intellectual underpinning. They felt that, in order to have credibility, Christianity needed to compete with Judaism and paganism on the intellectual front. While this of course provided a tremendous enriching of the Christian faith, it tipped the balance and intellectual theology won out over Jesus' message of love. Thus, the Church itself collaborated in the demythologizing and ultimately the de-spiritualizing of the West by privileging rational theology over Jesus' potent and transformative parabolic storytelling. Jesus' mystical life, his message of love and the miraculous healings he performed were all subordinated to the primacy of the institutional church, its intellectual theology, orthodoxy, doctrine and rules.

St Augustine's Doctrine of Original Sin

The third event that led Christianity ever further away from Christ's healing message of love was the introduction of the disastrous doctrine of 'original sin' by St Augustine. Augustine was a zealous convert to Christianity from Manicheism. He had a formidable intellect and became one of Christianity's greatest theologians. In converting to Christianity, he rejected the lasciviousness of his former life and embraced extreme moral rectitude, which informed his doctrine of original sin. He insisted that we are first and foremost sinners because we carry within us the 'original sin' of Eve and Adam. This quickly became a first principle of our essential self-identity, hammered home in Christian churches throughout Europe for almost two millennia – that we are fallen wrongdoers, fatally and justifiably separated from God through our own primordial wrongdoing.

Original sin is the singular travesty of Christian theology. It sets up an impossible-to-cross chasm between us and an already distant God. Life on Earth was deemed an exile; our finitude a deserved punishment; and any possible reconciliation with God could only occur, if at all, after we die. Our lives were meant to be a struggle. Our finitude, and our perceived separation, were our own fault and were pathological.

The attitude of the Church towards the people became one of an angry, masculine, chastising authority figure, justified in condoning, condemning, intimidating and oppressing the people, especially women. Obedience to the Church might help us to save our souls, and through the Church alone could we restore our broken relationship with God. The loving compassion of Jesus was subordinated to rules, regulations and chastisement. Instead of supporting us to live joyously as beings of love in love, Christianity taught us to live as broken and fallen sinners.

Augustine's legacy to Christianity also included a litany of dualisms that established fatal ruptures between all that he deemed good – God, heaven, the soul and reason – as against all that he deemed bad – humanity, Earth, the body and the senses. Christian dualism then married the dualism of reason, and these core beliefs of separation and resolute finitude became the foundation stones on which the whole edifice of Western culture and civilization was built. We were taught to believe in separation and division instead of wholeness and belonging. All of which contradicted in every way the gospel of Jesus, which taught love for one another – including even love for our enemies – and forgiveness of sins 'seventy times seven'.

Instead of embracing Jesus' maverick rejection of oppressive cultural, political and social norms, along with religious and institutional power structures, the early Church actively embraced those very elements. The power of Christianity grew hand in hand with the power of the Roman Empire. It fell into step with the march of reason, adopting and perpetuating the attendant splits between humanity and God; humanity and nature; and humanity against its own self. And worst of all, it set up a schism between the practice of spirituality and the practice of religion. As a result, the mystical essence of Jesus' teachings was lost to the very people for whom he had intended them.

The rituals, initiations and rites of passage inherent in Jesus' teaching, life and death were subordinated in favour of an intellectual teaching, which lost the sacred heart and the sacred energy of all that Jesus was trying to bring in for humanity. In a tragic irony, the Church itself contributed to the de-spiritualization of the West.

If, however, our creation myths and cultural and religious foundations had been anchored in a belief in wholeness, belonging, oneness, connection, mutual respect, reverence and awe – in practice and not just in theory – we would be living very different lives. If our civilization was founded on a belief in unity and love, as Jesus taught, what a different world we would be living in.

Acknowledging the necessarily abbreviated nature of this account of Christian history, I hope it nonetheless captures some of the key moments when things went wrong, and explains how it is that, 2,000 years later, my Catholic religion never once even came close to offering me – or anyone I know – appropriate spiritual guidance on the life-critical path of embodied spiritual awakening. Christianity, basing itself primarily in the intellect, lost its soul and its purpose. As a result, it lost touch with the very essence of Jesus' life and mission to guide people to an embodied experience of waking up to divine love.

Spiritual awakening is not and cannot be an intellectual experience. It is a lived, felt and embodied event. For Christians, it means to become Christ-ed, so that we feel ourselves to have become Christ-like and we live, or try very hard to live, as beings of love in love. But, the Church evolved in such a way that it abandoned its role as guardian of our spiritual awakening in favour of focusing on power, control, rules and regulations. The consequence has been followers simply walking away and looking elsewhere for the spiritual guidance we crave; or worse, abandoning the effort altogether.

The Rejection of Meditation and Mysticism

The next strand of our critique, and the one closest to my heart, is the wholesale and ongoing rejection by Christianity of meditation and mysticism for lay people. In doing so, it fails, refuses and neglects to teach, guide, facilitate or support depth-awakening to God as a natural life event. In my own case, it was left to my chance encounters with poets, philosophers, mystics and a craniosacral therapist to guide me through this most amazing life experience. My awakening happened outside of a religious context, in a philosophical context, yet, paradoxically, it brought me directly into the mystical love of Jesus that one ought to find blazing at the heart of a 'true Christianity'.

While I was of course grateful for the sometimes beautiful ceremonies, sacraments, rituals and exquisite music of my religious upbringing, none of it opened me to the depth of love and the true self-knowing that occurred almost immediately when I began to meditate. Without meditation, these rites and rituals inevitably stay at the level of the mind; and without mysticism, they are unlikely to lead to an embodied spiritual awakening.

My spiritual awakening turned out to be the most important experience of my whole life. It introduced a level of meaning that I had never even imagined was possible. Yet, the means to understand and process it all were hidden and veiled from me, like matches kept out of reach of a child. What we need now is a new, mature and robust mystical Christianity led by female and male mystics committed to supporting all of us to awaken. This new phase of Christianity for the third millennium should be organized in small local communities, decentralized from Rome, and must be led by mystic priestesses and priests who will support our full spiritual awakening to love as intended by Jesus.

THE ROLE OF MEDITATION

I had never known that incredible intimacy – union, even – with God is possible in meditation. I did not know that we are actually *meant* to experience this level of intimacy as our ongoing state of being once we wake up. Meditation naturally brings us to a much deeper place from which to live our lives. Inner peace arises naturally so that we become peaceful in ourselves, and bring peace with us wherever we go. Recently, I read that if all children were taught to meditate, we would have world peace within two generations. Why don't we do it?

If we are to live as children of the light, and as the beings of love, that Jesus tells us we are, then we must embody that self-knowing. No one can love from the mind, no matter how strong our intention or how complex our theology. Love must come from our heart, from the depths of who we know ourselves to be in our truth. It must come from an inner necessity to love, and from knowing that the whole purpose and meaning of life is to love. We must love because we cannot not love; just as Jesus loved us because he couldn't not love us; just as God loves us because God cannot not love us. In his whole being and nature, Jesus was love, and he tried to show us that we are, too. And the singular path to this wisdom is through meditation.

THE ROLE OF MYSTICISM

We all naturally have mystical experiences in our lives, whether we name them as such or not. They can occur in nature, or when reading poetry or while listening to music. We experience moments of stillness, of inexpressible beauty, of love, of peace – moments that allow us to feel that there is meaning and beauty, after all, in the whirl, and often the trauma, of life. We have a moment of consolation standing on a beach at sunset, or a moment of joy on hearing an exquisite piece of music, and this assures us that there is indeed something more than the chaos that surrounds us.

These experiences confirm our intuition of a whole, of a higher power, of God. They give a transient but powerfully affirming experience of the oneness of all in All. They carry us beyond the ordinary and the mundane to something unseen and ineffable, in which we sense the beautiful and the true.

There is a special flavour to the religious-mystical experience. The person is brought out of this world, to experience love and light directly. Their humanity dissolves and they burn in a fire of love, ecstatic to enter the light.

What life is inviting all of us to discover is that, behind and beyond our humanity, we are all in fact divine. Meister Eckhart taught that we are all *already* divine in our essential being because God placed a divine spark in each of us on our original creation. For this radical mysticism and for these exhilarating views on the intimacy of our relationship with God, Eckhart was convicted of heresy by Pope John XXII.

On the other hand, Thomas Aquinas, a near contemporary of Meister Eckhart who was maybe Christianity's greatest medieval theologian and a stalwart of orthodoxy, believed that the purpose of life is to *become* divine. Intuitively, I prefer Meister Eckhart's approach on the basis that in our original creation we are divine spiritual beings and cannot *not* be. But, in fact, it does not really matter which way we look at it, because the same spiritual work or commitment is needed to uncover either of those truths. Through our engagement with the development of our spiritual consciousness, we will either discover our divinity as a pre-existing fact, or our divinity will be revealed as the result of the spiritual work itself. A person who dies without having discovered they are already divine has missed the central meaning of life and Christianity must take much responsibility for this failure in the West.

There is an interesting aside about Thomas Aquinas, who contributed great intellectual riches to Christianity. Towards the end of his life, he received a divine revelation while celebrating Mass. After that vision, he said, 'The end of my labours has come. All that I have written appears to be as so much straw after the things that have been revealed to me.' Following that revelation, Aquinas refused to finish writing his masterpiece, the *Summa Theologica*. Yet it has been said that, 'Of this straw did Christianity proceed to make its bed.'

WE ARE ALL CALLED TO MYSTICISM

Jesus was the supreme exemplar of the mystic life. He was the mystic of mystics and the archetypal mystic. Christians believe he was the Son of God, one with God in every way. The essence of his incarnation, life, death and resurrection were mystical events of the highest order. His life was the mystic event upon which Christianity was founded, yet somehow this burning heart of the Christ Way was lost by the very people who assumed responsibility for protecting it.

The mystic experience comes first; organized religion second. Jesus, mystic extraordinaire, *is* the foundation for Christianity. Just as the mystic experience of Abraham is the foundation for Judaism, and the mystic experience of Muhammad is the foundation for Islam. Mysticism comes first, religion second. If each of these religions had been true to its *raison d'être*, it would have made mysticism central to all that it does, but instead each of them replaced the exquisite, ineffable, majestic, sacred, transcendent mystic way with the cold, and often lacerating, way of the law.

The institutional Christian Church as good as stripped the religion of its mystical fire. Yet, what else was Jesus but a *mystic*? What else was his mother, Mary, but a mystic? What else was Mary Magdalene but a mystic? What else was John the Beloved, who wrote the only recorded mystic gospel, but a mystic? The New Testament, and other gospels excluded from it, such as the gospel of Mary Magdalene, are brimming with accounts of the mystical events and experiences of Jesus' life and community. What else were Jesus' disciples, female and male, and his followers far and wide, but mystics-in-training? And what else are we called to, as humans and as lovers of Christ, but mysticism?

In suppressing the centrality of mysticism in the early Christ community, the depth and the wealth of what a true Christianity had to offer was lost. Every wisdom system and religion of the world has a mystical dimension that could contribute a unique dimension to our understanding and experience of God. For the Christian mystic, that dimension is love. The failure to bring mysticism into mainstream religious practice in the West constitutes a radical failure by our religions.

My deep belief now is that we are all called to this mystical level of being, and that there is an urgency to realizing it. It is this mystical awareness of the oneness of all in love that will help us to save ourselves, our species and our planet. Anyone embodying the mystical mind will necessarily be living from love, peace, harmony, compassion, justice and equality: the mystic cannot tolerate violations of the higher ideals and will be driven to speak out against them, each in our own best way, true to our natural talents and gifts, as part of our life's work.

In return for my mystic gift, I gave to God the gifts of my career and of my writing. I abandoned my efforts to get my precious novel published and I placed my writing fully in the service of bringing in all that I now know of God as nothing but love. And, by the remarkable blessing of life, the first effort I made to get this book published was successful.

THE CANONICAL REJECTION OF FEMALE WRITING

The last mis-step we will look at here is the one taken by Christianity, again in the 4th century, when choosing the books that would be included in the canonical Bible. In doing so, they ignored entirely the contribution of female writers to Christian writing and thinking. They deliberately left out the female perspective, insight, expression and understanding of the Christ experience. Are we to believe that no women were capable of writing or contributing the feminine perspective of Jesus' life and teachings? The most egregious omission was of course the omission of the Gospel of Mary Magdalene, the existence of which we now have definitive proof. Of the many iconoclastic behaviours by Jesus, one of the most radical was his egalitarian treatment of women, such that he drew no distinction between men and women in his ministry of love.

Was not his beloved Mary Magdalene the first apostle to whom Jesus revealed his risen form? And did not Jesus appear to her *twice* on that first day? And didn't Jesus ask *her to* tell the others that he had risen? Yet, her privileged telling of this most sacred event was usurped by the male disciples, who subsumed her experience into the telling of their own stories. The loss of the female voice and experience to early Christianity is a travesty that blights the religion to this day. The deliberate exclusion of the feminine has damaged the whole fabric of Christianity, and also of Western culture, giving an unbalanced, exclusively male perspective that bolsters the supposed justification for the all-male clergy.

Mary Magdalene has said to me on many occasions in my visions and locutions: 'Speak for me as I was not allowed to speak.' Here, I am doing my best to speak for her.

Leonardo da Vinci's 'The Last Supper' shows the disciples gathered with Jesus for their last supper before his crucifixion. It is painted as a mural onto the refectory wall of a convent that miraculously survived bombing during World War II. The painting had always been presumed to depict the male disciples until recent analysis by art experts proved that the disciple closest to Jesus, and leaning into him, was in fact painted as a woman, and is presumed to be Mary Magdalene.

It is my absolute understanding, from all that I have experienced in my mystical journey, that Jesus had a group of close female disciples, mirroring the group of his male disciples. I believe these women gathered in their own community and were equally anointed by the Holy Spirit on Pentecost with the gift of speech, but their letters, their teaching and their wisdom was deliberately excluded.

In compiling the Bible from an exclusively masculine telling of the life and teachings of Jesus, we are given a one-sided male, patriarchal perspective. Thus, early Christianity fed and perpetuated the oppression of women already practised in Greek and Roman civilizations, where women were lower than slaves on the social ladder. In this and other ways, Christianity contributed to the creation of a society in which women continue to be second-class citizens in the world today.

THE FUTURE OF CHRISTIANITY

If Christianity and the other Western faiths are to survive, if they are to have any relevance for this third millennium, they must also transform. Christianity must meditate deeply on Jesus' call to love, and on how it might better lead its people into a true consciousness of our inherent divinity, of our inner light and of our being as love. Until Christianity embraces meditation and mysticism as central elements on the path to God, it has almost nothing real to offer those who would wake up to divine love as a natural life event and as an embodied, lived experience in life.

If I were Pope, I would immediately dismantle the whole organization, reflect deeply on how to reconfigure it as a living expression of the mystical love of Jesus and only start again when prepared to walk in humble partnership with the people towards a global awakening to love. As I said in the Introduction, what Jesus is calling for today is a conversion of Christianity to a New Christianity of Love. However, we do not have time to wait for the institutional Christian Church to take the action that is urgently needed, so we must take the initiative ourselves, trusting in the immediate guidance of Jesus, Mother Mary, Mary Magdalene, the Holy Spirit and whichever other divinities offer their spiritual guidance to us.

World peace depends on all of us committing to meditation. The future of humanity depends on all of us opening to the mystic. The health of Mother Earth, and the future of life, depends on both. Just as the Earth urgently needs to be re-wilded and her forests re-forested, life and our lives need to be re-spiritualized, re-mythologized and re-enchanted.

MOVING TO A NARRATIVE OF LOVE

What is now urgently needed is to overturn the narrative of separation and replace it with a narrative of love. We must replace the dualistic mindset of division and separation with a mindset of belonging, communion, harmony, peace and oneness in love. We must undo the psychological disposition towards separation and division that infects our culture, and replace it with something radically holistic that allows us to know ourselves, as always and ever, deeply and inseparably, belonging to the divine intelligence of love.

We need a new founding story, one that truly interprets the meaning of what God inscribed into our very being, on our original creation. Our new story must be a story of love; one that tells us that we are beings of love, made by love, out of love, for love and in love. With this as our guiding premise, we will then naturally live in love.

It is perfectly clear to me, on first principles, that there was no fall, no original sin and no separation. We have been fundamentally mistaken about the nature of God; about our own true nature; and about the nature of our relationship with God.

If we are to turn things around – as urgently we must – if we are to save our species, and our beautiful planet, we need a complete and total transformation of our consciousness; even a 'metanoia', meaning a radical and fundamental change at the very depths of who we know ourselves to be. We need to move from a mindset of separation and division to one of wholeness and oneness in love. We need to adopt this as our new self-knowing, and grow into higher consciousness, otherwise humanity will continue on its downwards spiral towards imminent self-extinction –

the first species ever to orchestrate its own extinction. If we do not, then humanity may very well become extinct without ever having known that its whole meaning and purpose was to wake up – to transcend its natural finitude here and now, and to enter love as the highest possible expression of life.

In the next chapter I offer an alternative founding story that is anchored in wholeness, belonging and love. It offers a benevolent explanation for the apparent separation between us and God by suggesting that our perception of separation in fact points to the whole meaning and purpose of human life. My new understanding is that engaging meaningfully with this perception of separation is the very path that leads us from the darkness of not knowing we belong to the light to the revelation that we do in fact belong, and must inexorably belong, eternally as light in the Light and as love in Love.

~

CHAPTER 14

BECOMING DIVINE

There is no separation; there never was.

From the very beginning, humanity has been marked by a frustration with its finitude. We yearn to transcend our limits – to do more, to be more and to know more than appears possible. Our feelings of curiosity and frustration prompt us to journey into the unknown. It is not difficult to interpret this frustration as a purposeful part of our design intended to push us beyond apparent limits. Aristotle said, a long time ago, that, 'All [people] by nature desire to know.'

Our greatest frustration is, of course, with finitude itself. We long for transcendence. What if this, too, is designed to prompt us to proceed not just beyond physical and intellectual limits, but also beyond finitude itself and into immediate relationship with God? What if our core feeling of being lost, abandoned and separated from God – our inability to understand the meaning of life, our frustration with our finitude and our seemingly futile yearning for transcendence – was precisely and exactly the plan?

What if the plan all along was for us to live a life that is exquisitely designed to facilitate the move from experiencing ourselves as being lost to being found; of moving from darkness to the light; from ignorance to knowing; from chaos to order; from the physical to the spiritual; from apparent separation to the joy of union – and all while we still live in this physical space-time universe? In other words, what if the plan all along was for us to wake up?

A New Axial Age

This is exactly what I now think the design of humanity has been moving towards all along, and has in fact reached in our day. It is a very naive person who thinks that evolution has climaxed with the rational human being. I think that we are once more in a moment of profound evolutionary shift, a new Axial Age, and that we are moving into the New Age of Love. I think that life is a gift that, so far, we have failed to understand. I think our core frustration holds within it precisely the seeds of our potential for transcendence – here and now – and this is how we can create heaven on our beautiful planet Earth. But instead of following this trajectory to create heaven on Earth, we have set about manufacturing something much closer to hell.

Life is clearly set up for us to move through three levels of growth and development: to move from physical-biological, to psychological and intellectual growth. From there we are meant to proceed to our spiritual growth. Except that we do not. Our culture is stuck. At best, it is stuck at level two; at worst, it is still at level one.

We do not know how to proceed with ease beyond the egoic concerns of the second phase of our psychological-intellectual development. We are spinning in a vortex of self-interest at the level of egoic, material, psychological and intellectual concerns, frustratedly amassing more of the same, distracting ourselves with different versions of the same, and all without satisfaction. We do not know how to catapult into the next natural phase of our spiritual growth and development. We are like a spaceship endlessly circling a planet awaiting the powerful boost needed to slingshot it into the next orbit.

It was in reflecting deeply on these conundrums of life that a beautiful idea finally came into my mind with the force of truth and pointed me at last to the paradox that lies at the heart of the human experience: God, in its infinite creativity, designed us to be temporarily finite beings, explicitly to discover that we are not finite. God designed us to perceive ourselves as separate, explicitly to discover that we are not separate. We start off 'asleep' in order to have the phenomenal experience of 'waking up'. When this idea came into my mind, it set my whole being on fire. At last there was an explanation for how we are that does not involve punishment and sin.

Here is the miracle: our finitude was intended to be temporary, even within the overall temporality of human life itself.

Our suffering comes from not understanding this and from resigning ourselves to seemingly insuperable finitude, accepting chaos, accepting disorder, accepting ignorance, accepting being lost, accepting the darkness, and living as if we are separate and alone, rather than beautiful parts of a beautiful whole. Our suffering comes from a limited understanding of God, or from living as if there is no power greater than ourselves; as if we brought ourselves into existence, as if this exquisite planet just happens to be perfectly positioned in our galaxy for life to thrive at this time, and as if by some remarkable chance the first single-celled organism, through some as yet unfathomable method, self-replicated and started biological life on Earth.

Spiritual growth and awakening are absolutely coded into our original design – we are made for it. The proof lies in experiencing it – we can only know it by living it. Not to experience spiritual awakening as a natural milestone in life is grossly to have missed the whole point of life. If we could catapult out of our level-two living into mature spiritual seeking from a place of love, humanity would finally be able to come into its own meaning, purpose and full actualization, which paradoxically *is* transcendence.

One of Aristotle's greatest insights was to determine that all being moves from potential to actuality. He called the impulse – the active principle that draws out the potential into actuality – the *entelekheia*, or entelechy. One way to understand the entelechy of something is to think of it as the consciousness of the actualized form bringing itself from its state of potential into its actualized form or manifest existence.

For example, the butterfly is the entelechy of the caterpillar. The rose is the entelechy of the rose seed. The oak tree is the entelechy of the acorn. The entelechy of the butterfly draws the butterfly out of the caterpillar, just as the entelechy of the rose draws the rose out of the rose seed, and just as the entelechy of the oak tree draws the tree out of the acorn.

In our case, our entelechy is our fully expressed, fully actualized, human-spiritual self. In our time, our entelechy now calls us to self-transcendence or spiritual-mystical awakening. When we become who we truly are, we flourish and feel ourselves to be deeply and incomparably alive and fulfilled in life. We enter the fullest and most authentic expression of who we truly are. This is the paradox Heidegger spoke about when he wrote, 'Become who you already are.'

The potential to become our best selves is already in us, and our entelechy is consciously trying to draw out our fullest, most authentic self-expression. At the same time, our entelechy is also pushing us to become our truest self. Our entelechy knows what it is trying to achieve – and our job is not to block it. What Aristotle called the entelechy is really the vision God holds of us in our original spiritual creation.

Our awakening lays the foundation for us to live our best and most authentic lives, to come into our highest meaning and deepest purpose, and to become who we came here to be.

Humanity itself also has an entelechy and a highest flourishing – which Aristotle called *eudaemonia* – wherein we actualize the fullest expression of what we are as a species. The entire purpose of human life is to become whole in mind, body and spirit, through a co-creative relationship between ourselves, nature and God. We need to transcend our finitude, and to feel ourselves come home most beautifully to the oneness of all in love. In other words, quite simply, to wake up and create heaven on Earth. As Aristotle intuited 2,300 years ago, we are meant to change, and to change utterly, as a caterpillar changes into a butterfly. We are meant to become almost unrecognizable to our finite selves, and to know that manifesting our inner beauty and joy in God is the actualized truth of who we are as a species.

ENTERING THE LIGHT OF LOVE

We are the species that can bring creation full circle, back to God. We do this by entering our spiritual maturity, by transcending our finitude and coming into unity-consciousness, by coming to know God in rapture and in ecstasy, and by entering the light that is love, even while we are still human.

We are a bridge between the created universe and God. We are an in-between species, designed specifically to move between the material and the spiritual realms; between our finitude and infinitude. This is the whole point and purpose of humanity. We are designed to know our creator while still in finite material form. The implications of this are mind-blowing – that the highest purpose of human life is specifically to have the lived experience of coming to know God while still in human form and then to live from that enlightened consciousness in every moment of our mature adult lives. This is what the New Age of Love now offers to us.

What greater experience could God design for a conscious species like us than the experience of *temporarily* not knowing our deep, profound and indissoluble belonging to God, for the exact purpose of *crossing over* from this temporary not knowing into an eternal knowing of this ecstatic truth? What greater experience could God offer than the gift of the blazing joy it is to move from darkness to light, from ignorance to divine knowing, from finitude to infinitude, from ordinary life to ecstasy? And not as an optional extra, but as the whole point and purpose of life.

And this explains why we are born with free will – we can only experience these incredible events if we *choose* them. So, our biggest mistake is to live as if our finitude and our separation are insurmountable, whereas in fact we are designed for transcendence, for infinitude and for mystical union with God.

TO CREATE HEAVEN ON EARTH

It was *we* who introduced ideas of brokenness, separation and being fallen. We were impatient to understand, and we rushed to mistaken conclusions. It is not that we have a fallen nature but that we have an impatient nature. I believe it is precisely God's plan for us humans, in this coming era, to recreate heaven in the physical-material plane – to make a heaven of this incredibly beautiful Earth. This is the plan.

Waking up to divine love represents not just a perfectly natural phase of life, but the most beautiful and meaningful one of all. We come into the most exquisite feeling of homecoming, belonging, joy, peace and stillness. The search for meaning is now over; the journey is complete, and we start living as beings of light in love. As T.S. Eliot wrote, 'We shall not cease from exploration, and the end of all our exploring will be to arrive where we started and know the place for the first time.'

Anyone who experiences this joy of moving into spiritual maturity knows with absolute certainty that this is what life is all about. This at last answers our desperate need to belong, to find wholeness, to be found, to reach certainty, to have deep meaning and purpose in our lives, to reach journey's end and to enter intimate relationship with God. And when we do, we know that there is nothing in the known or unknown multiverses that could possibly be greater than this golden homecoming to the light. This patently is the meaning of life – to be on fire with love in the light.

When all this became clear in my mind, I was absolutely certain that there was no separation and there was no fall, but there was a misunderstanding. There was a mistaken belief in a fall, and *this* has distorted our sense of self. Instead of perceiving ourselves as belonging beautifully to a harmonious whole, as beautiful parts of beautiful creation, we instead perceive ourselves to be lost in a rat race of dog eat dog. In a desperate bid for survival at any cost, we perceive 'others' as the enemy rather than as a friend. I have concluded, therefore, as I have mentioned before, with both joy and sadness: *life is a gift that tragically we have failed to understand.*

What we now need is a fundamental and radical overhaul of the foundational premise of Western civilization: we are not separate, we are not fallen, but we are fundamentally mistaken in our self-understanding. We have interpreted as our own fault our perceived separateness and division from each other and from the unifying principle we call God. We wrongly perceived this as being fatal and irreversible in this life, rather than recognizing it as central to the plan of creation all along.

It is this singular belief in separation that now lies at the root of all hate, injustice, inequality, dis-ease and killing. God designed the human species as one among billions, precisely to give us the experience of coming home to love beyond the space-time continuum while we still live within it. That is the miracle of life. Just as a flower is gifted with the joy of blossoming in spring, or the sunset to blaze in fiery colours across the Atlantic skyline, humans are gifted with the potential to create and experience the joy of heaven on Earth while still human. What more do we want?

The path from darkness to light is precisely the intended trajectory of life, through the journey of physical, psychological and spiritual maturity. Spiritual awakening is precisely the process to complete our growth so that we transcend our finitude and discover the blazing power of light and love at the centre of ourselves and all of life. In discovering the light while we are still human, we learn to look with new eyes and a new heart – and if our broken species could learn to do this now, we would quickly create a new humanity, and a whole new world.

Like God, we, too, are creators, and the highest and greatest thing we could ever create is peace on Earth by living lives of love. When more and more of us accept this vision of our true nature, the word can spread like fire across the globe – that the absolute meaning and the absolute purpose of life is absolute love.

We are beautiful parts of beautiful creation. There is no separation and there never was.

~

CHAPTER 15

THE PATH OF GOLD: A GUIDE TO AWAKENING

'You and I share one heart and one love. I am you, you are me, we are one. I AM the Beating Heart of Love at the centre of all existence.'

JESUS

We arrive now at the beating heart of this book of love. Here, I will bring together all that I have learned of the process of waking up to divine love in a way that I hope will be helpful and of service to readers who want to engage with their own awakening.

Transcending our finitude and dissolving the perception of separation is the very process of waking up to divine love. We transcend our finitude by accepting the invitation into transcendence. And we heal our perception of separation by opening to the inherent connection of all to All. The question is: how do we do this? The paradoxical answer is: we do not do anything. Rather, we let it be 'done' to us. As I have emphasized throughout, waking up is a natural life process that has its own inner intelligence, energetics, laws and dynamics. It knows what it wants to do and it knows how to do it. Our job is not to block it. We must re-learn how to let our awakening happen; re-learn how to surrender to being led through the transformation of our consciousness by divine love. Our job is to cooperate, collaborate and co-create with God in the experience of our own awakening.

Waking up begins when we allow God to effect the transformation of our ordinary consciousness into a spiritual consciousness of love. We allow ourselves to be re-formed in love, by love. In the first half of life we enjoy our independence, as seeming masters of our own lives; the second half of life is when we realize our intimate belonging to God. We allow ourselves to be guided into spiritual consciousness, in preparation for the final homecoming when we fully return to the womb of love. In the second half of life, God reaches out the hand of love, inviting us into a divine dance, and it is up to us whether we will join in or not.

THE WAY OF PARADOX

Everything about waking up, and about shifting into spiritual consciousness, is counterintuitive and paradoxical. We are entering a liminal space, transitioning from reason to spirit, moving into an unfamiliar realm where different intelligence, energies and dynamics are in play. We must re-learn how to be in this new and unusual space.

Moving from the intellectual to the spiritual means that the tools of the rational mind, such as logic, reasoning and making plans, are no longer any help to us; in fact, they actively hinder, block and delay the process. Analysing our awakening with the rational mind keeps us stuck at the intellectual level and prevents us from being opened to the level of spirit. We must let go of the need to know intellectually what is going on because the intellect is quite simply the wrong faculty for this experience. We are not abandoning the intellect, just recognizing that a different type of intelligence now needs to take the lead.

For spiritual growth we must embrace the way of paradox and unknowing, and we must learn to work with the spiritual tools of intuition, silence, receptivity, passivity, surrender, trust, curiosity, awe and, most of all, humility. This is the way of love. The essence of the awakening mind is the ability to hold paradox; to accept apparent contradictions without getting upset; and to accept that things may not be as they seem to be to the rational mind. It is to become comfortable with unknowing, to allow our consciousness to expand and to develop new capacities.

The awakening mind operates primarily through feeling. We want to *feel* the rightness of all that is unfolding; we want to feel it in the depths of our being; so that we know, without knowing how we know, that we are on the right path. This requires great humility. Awakening is a living process – we surrender our need to know 'the how', and open ourselves to being led.

The Seven Stages of Awakening

From analysing the milestones on my own path to awakening I was able to identify seven universal stages of the awakening process. The seven stages are:

1. The call to awaken and interpret the signs of spiritual dis-ease

2. The journey within

3. The liminal space and the consciousness of longing

4. Transmission from an awakened mind and reading the mystics

5. Unity consciousness

6. The consciousness of the divinity of all creation

7. Spiritual-mystical consciousness or divine union

Awakening as Living Process

Awakening is a living process with its own rhythm and energy. We do not schedule our awakening, and nor does it follow a strict timetable or a rigid linear structure. We do not tick a box and move on to the next phase. While the first and the seventh stages of awakening are definitive, the ones in between will unfold in a fluid spiral-like fashion, so we need to be open to the living movement of our awakening. The stages I am sharing here are the archetypal milestones of the development of spiritual consciousness, and the methods are universally true, but awakening will be a unique experience for each different person. What I am sharing is a gentle guide in the context of a living process. It is a guide to help us become familiar with what is in play. It is a map of the spiritual terrain, but it is not prescriptive as to how you must walk it. I am just hoping to expand our understanding so that we can engage meaningfully with a natural process. Awakening can take years – it took me 46 and counting – so do not put pressure on yourself to be achieving certain ends within a certain timeframe, because that is contrary to the whole spirit of what we are about. Rather, just be open and, most of all, be curious!

STAGE ONE: THE CALL TO AWAKEN

Awakening begins with a spiritual call, when life itself calls us into our highest actualization and self-transcendence. Self-actualization concerns what we think brings the greatest fulfilment to our lives, whereas self-transcendence occurs when we let God show us how to live from and for our highest good in co-creation with life and love itself.

The spiritual call begins at that time in life when, despite meeting the given markers of success, we still feel empty. Despite achieving well in our career and having successful personal relationships; despite being fulfilled as the mother or father we might always have longed to be; despite having material comfort and a place to call home; despite all these things, or maybe because we have none of them, we feel empty. Our life lacks meaning and no longer has any true sense of purpose.

We feel that there is something more we should be doing with our life, but we do not know what it is. We want to have a greater sense of meaning and purpose but we are unsure how to achieve this. We no longer feel satisfied with our life but we do not know how to get it back on track.

We may begin to have moods of anxiety but are not sure why we are anxious. We may sometimes have a sense of becoming detached from ordinary life, so that life does not feel real anymore. We may feel disconnected from ourselves and the world around us. We may start to feel a generalized malaise that has no focus. We feel stuck and off track. And most of all, we may find ourselves overwhelmed by a longing for something vast but we have no idea what it is.

On the outside, our lives may look the way they are meant to look, but on the inside, things feel very wrong.

On one reading, these feelings could all be interpreted as (and often are mistaken for) an archetypal midlife crisis. But the difference is that, no matter what we do at the material-psychological-intellectual level, the feelings do not get resolved. Things at the lower level of ego consciousness – such as a new job, a new partner, a new house, a new country, a new hobby or a holiday – are no longer enough to satisfy these feelings. Whereas previously we might have embraced psychotherapy, taken up a new skill or even turned to alcohol, for example, these things no longer answer to the depth of our discontent. They may temporarily mask the feelings, but the feelings will gnaw away just below the surface, because the time has come when something more radical is needed in our life. Self-actualization is no longer enough; we are now being called to self-transcendence.

I call these feelings the archetypal signs of spiritual dis-ease, because they are signalling precisely to us that we are ready to shift into our mature spiritual development. The dis-ease we feel is letting us know that we are ready for the 'more' that lies beyond the egoic-intellectual-psychological phase of life. The feelings are actively telling us that we are ready to awaken. Consequently, we must develop a new way of responding and engaging with them so that they can guide us towards our awakening.

THE SIGNS OF SPIRITUAL DIS-EASE

~ We feel there is something missing from our lives but we do not know what it is.

~ We no longer feel fulfilled despite having reached supposed markers of success in life.

~ We feel discontent but we do not know why.

~ We sense that we are off track in our careers or in some other fundamental way.

~ We experience generalized anxiety that has no focus.

~ We feel empty despite having a seemingly full life.

~ We are frustrated with life but we are not sure why.

~ We long for something but we do not know what it is.

~ We feel there is something we are meant to be doing with our lives but again we do not know what it is.

And most crucially of all:

~ We feel that our life is losing its meaning and its purpose.

INTERPRETING THE SIGNS OF SPIRITUAL DIS-EASE

At all costs, we must resist the instinct to respond to these feelings with the rational mind. Instead, we need to adopt the completely opposite approach of curiosity, wonder and, ultimately, surrender. It is critical to appreciate that our feelings of frustration and longing are not rational or psychological responses to life's circumstances. *They are their own unique event of spiritual dis-ease.* They are meaningful in their own particular way, and the way to understand them is to surrender to them. We must make ourselves vulnerable before life, and allow *it* to guide us into its mysteries.

The feelings themselves are the call to awaken. God is now orchestrating the double event of calling us by causing us to feel these feelings in the first place. We are not used to this type of event in our lives, but when we remember that God is pure intelligence, this should help us to trust in what is happening.

We must now allow ourselves to be led by God, by intelligence and by love into our higher self.

Two crucial observations need to be made here, right at the outset, which will set the scene for everything that follows. The first is to notice that all of the feelings listed previously can be placed into two categories: frustration and longing. The second is to notice that none of these feelings has an object. Both of these observations are highly significant. I really invite you to pause here... to go slowly with these observations... let them sink in... treat them as important truths, because something very different is now in play.

FRUSTRATION AND LONGING

I encourage you to let what follows touch your heart... that behind these various expressions of frustration lie powerful and deeper truths:

— Behind our frustration is a deep-seated frustration with finitude;

— Behind our longing is a longing for transcendence.

These two truths will guide the rest of this journey. The entire path to awakening lies in navigating this frustration and responding to this longing in a new way.

FEELINGS WITH NO OBJECT

The most unusual characteristic of the signs of spiritual dis-ease is that they have no object. We do not know what we long for; we do not know why we are frustrated; we do not know what would give meaning to our lives. The reason for this is because finite things of the finite world are no longer enough for us. We are ready for 'more' in every way.

Our old way of being in the world cannot help us here. We must find a new way forwards. The intellect needs an object to work with, but here there is no object. The paradox is that if we approach these feelings in the right way, the feelings themselves will tell us what they want for us, and even more so, what they are offering to us.

These feelings of frustration contain within them the very sign that we are ready for transcendence – that our consciousness is ripe for transformation. The sense of yearning and longing that we feel is life itself drawing us into the next stage of our development; it is our entelechy drawing out our potential for transcendence. We need to let our spiritual-self come forwards now and let it show us the way.

When we embark on this journey, we need to be open to being surprised, because we will come out on the far side changed utterly in our being, and maybe our lives will be changed utterly, too – so let us not resist, but instead surrender to all that is involved in this crucial transformation, just as a caterpillar surrenders to its own metamorphosis into a butterfly.

In my own experience, discovering that these feelings were meaningful did not mean that I then understood what they meant. Instinctively, however, I knew that my rational mind was no longer of any help to me. I abandoned all intellectual effort to understand and intuitively opened to the unknown.

THE SHIFT INTO UNKNOWING

Moving into the liminal space is precisely the step that is needed for developing our spiritual consciousness. It may seem frightening to let go of the intellect, to step off into the unknown, to let go of all markers of self-knowing and self-understanding, but it is crucial. Until we do so, the process is stalled. It is a paradox that beyond the intellect lies a higher form of knowing called 'unknowing'. Historically, unknowing has been the meeting ground for the mystic with God. But we need to realize that it is the meeting ground for everybody with God. We are all called to be mystics and to step off into the unknown. The paradox is that the attitude of unknowing is precisely what leads us into a new and a higher type of knowing.

THE NEW APPROACH USING SPIRITUAL TOOLS

Approaching these feelings in a new way requires a new stance and a new attitude. The new approach is a spiritual approach with appropriate spiritual tools, which are: prayer, intuition, curiosity, wonder, passivity, receptivity, trust and surrender. These all constitute the appropriate methodology for engaging with our awakening. They are the keys to unlocking our spiritual consciousness.

We are not, of course, talking of ordinary curiosity here, such as, 'I wonder what will happen?' This is depth curiosity at the level of the soul. This is wonder that opens us up at the core of our being. This is intuition at the level of the energies of life – reading them, sensing them, listening to them and interpreting them. Our passivity has an active quality, so that we are not sitting idly by, waiting for things to happen: rather, we are receptive to what is coming, akin to premonition, or heightened awareness; we are anticipating what is coming our way, and preparing to co-create our future selves with the divine.

We prepare to surrender, but our surrender is not a hopeless succumbing: rather, we paradoxically step forward courageously, to welcome whatever it is that life is offering. We radically detach from wanting specific outcomes. We expect nothing but are prepared for everything. We try not to block what is coming in. We allow the deepest meaning and the highest purpose of our lives now to surface in us. We begin to discern the way forwards by listening and sensing with our whole being to whatever it is we hear calling to us. And in all this, we proceed with complete humility.

We are trying to open up a sacred space both within ourselves and within our lives in which we can begin to hear the voice of love, calling us home, by our own name. Here is something interesting: when love calls us by our name, it is calling us into our highest self-expression, our highest authenticity, our highest meaning and purpose. Love is calling us to become who we came here to be. If in my truth I am a spiritual writer, that version of me is what will now naturally come forward in my life. If you, in your truth, are a gardener, a herbalist, a yoga teacher, an entrepreneur or whatever – that is the version of you that will now be called forth. So we need to engage spiritually, prayerfully, reverently and energetically with the energy of these feelings that are pushing us to grow into who we are in our truth.

We want to sit with these feelings with reverence. We want to take them into prayer and meditation; into nature and to sacred sites; into special places where we love to go, places where wonder naturally arises, places where we can feel sacred energies. And then we simply want to *be* with our feelings. We are trying to let *them* show us the way forwards. So, we open ourselves to signs, feelings in our bodies, coincidences, doors opening, new paths opening up, opportunities coming our way. The new approach is to be in wonder and curiosity, open and receptive. Of all the spiritual tools, surrender and meditation are the most important, and so they now deserve their own section.

STAGE TWO: THE JOURNEY WITHIN

SURRENDER, MEDITATION, DETACHMENT

The central practice we need to develop if we are to make any progress on the spiritual path is to cultivate the art of stillness through meditation. Meditation starts as a method, which paradoxically becomes the path, and then a way of life. It is both a practice and a stage of awakening. Meditation is the foundation stone of transformation. It is the single most powerful practice in the entire awakening process. In meditation, we are creating a sacred space for God to communicate with us. We are creating the fertile conditions in which this may begin to happen. God communicates through silence, and will never try to compete with the noise of the world to get our attention. Therefore, if we want to be in communication with that sacred energy, if we want to hear life's call, if we want to hear love calling us by our name, we must learn how to be truly silent and still, and then to trust in what we 'hear'.

'You find me in the Stillness
because I AM the Stillness.'
VOICE OF GOD

MEDITATION AS A SACRED PRACTICE

The absolute essence of meditation is for us to cultivate a sense of awe before the sacred. There are innumerable meditation teachers, methods, practices, techniques and traditions, but behind the success of each different one lies the imperative of being able to surrender. The greater our capacity to surrender, the more effective will be the particular technique we practise. Surrender lays the foundation for successful meditation, and our surrender now is not just to the liminal space, but it is also surrender to God.

I encourage everyone to treat meditation as the sacred practice it is. We are seeking to enter a sacred space, we are seeking to enter the presence of God, and so we should approach meditation with due reverence and respect. We mark it out as a holy time in our day, and acknowledge the sacredness of what we are engaged in.

In order to cultivate a sense of awe before the sacred it is a good idea to create an altar of sorts – even something as simple as lighting a candle to mark the fact that we are opening ourselves to be in the presence of God. We are inviting God to come to us, and if we want to experience an energetic shift into the sacred during the meditation, we need to prepare for it. As an example, I always remove my shoes for meditation, taking my cue from the Book of Exodus, in which God said to Moses during the episode of the burning bush: 'Remove the sandals from your feet for you are on holy ground.' The more we can acknowledge that meditation is a sacred practice, that we are stepping onto holy ground, the more sacred it will become. We should treat meditation with the same reverence as if we were entering a holy shrine, a pilgrim site, a church or a place of worship.

It is a good idea to begin with a prayer, to bless our meditation and invoke the protection of the highest light of love. We then consciously hand ourselves over to our special spiritual guides, Mother-Father God, or whatever holy name we prefer to invoke. Having blessed the experience in this way, we can safely trust that whatever may unfold will be holy, trustworthy and for our highest good.

MEDITATION AS SURRENDER TO GOD

In meditation, our surrender is to God. We still ourselves so completely that we open a space for God to communicate directly with us. Here again, we encounter a paradox – we want to meet God, but to do so, we must do nothing. Meeting God is not like setting out to meet a friend for dinner; instead, we prepare a space *inside us* for God to come *to us*.

We invite God in, without having the slightest idea how God will visit, or if we will even be aware of the visit. We move beyond prayer, into nothingness, and sit in ever more profound stillness. When we do so, somehow, in sacred silence, God enters. We feel a presence, stillness, peace or joy, and we know, without knowing how, that God is with us. Maybe a fire will begin to burn in us, maybe we will 'see' the light at the centre of our being, maybe we will see the light outside us, maybe we will hear the voice of God, maybe we will feel certain sensations in our body, or maybe nothing at all. Either way, we trust that God has been with us.

The whole purpose of meditation is to allow ourselves to be transformed – not instantly but incrementally, over time, and as we do, our outer lives improve in so many ways. Meditation reshapes our whole way of being in the world. Through meditation we achieve inner peace. Meditation is to our spiritual wellbeing what sleep is to our physical, psychological, emotional and intellectual wellbeing – imperative. Without meditation, nothing will change.

You may recall my own naivety when I first began to meditate: I created a little altar with flowers, a candle and a photo of my father. I sat at my kitchen table, closed my eyes and became still. Unknowingly, I was opening to the divine, and love itself came flooding in. This simple practice is still my primary method of meditation: nothing else – no breathing technique, no mantras, no method. Nothing other than stillness, surrender and no expectation that anything in particular will happen, but also open to whatever might actually happen.

Sometimes in meditation an idea, image or a word comes to mind that draws us into a creative visualization. This is not the same as our mind simply wandering, because it has a different energetic quality to it. Over time we learn to distinguish between the two, so that we can ignore the first but surrender to the second. When this happens to me in meditation, I surrender to that prompt and I am sometimes brought on profound inner visions and experiences. I do not create these experiences; I surrender to them. We should never chase an experience in meditation, rather just let what happens, happen, but I would love to offer an example of what I am talking about by sharing the experience I had in a recent morning meditation. It is a lived experience of what I am trying to explain.

A Lived Experience of Surrender

I sat at my desk in my study and lit a candle and a stick of frankincense. I put on Hildegard of Bingen's 'O Virtus Sapientiae' at very low volume, on repeat, on my phone, and set the timer for 20 minutes. Then I closed my eyes and sat very still. Soon I felt myself sink into deep stillness. From there, I lost all awareness of myself, the music, the incense and my study. This is what I wrote in my journal afterwards:

'In my inner seeing, I am brought to the edge of the Atlantic Ocean. I feel the sublime stillness and peace of the west of Ireland come over me. The expanse of ocean stretches out before me, and I feel the vastness of space and time all around. Slowly, I begin to feel the stillness of Being itself, and I am filled with peace.

'I feel deeply loved, and I want to reach out to touch this love. I want to embrace it. But there is nothing to touch, and nothing to embrace. And so, I realize that I am being touched, that I am being embraced, by love itself. Then I surrender my whole self; and my being dissolves into formless love. I lose all particularity and I dissolve, as if into infinite particles which then dissipate into love, like air, into air.

'Then I float in the being of love and I am quietly ecstatic.

'So deeply do I feel myself in the stillness of the being of love that I know the entire physical universe could evaporate and it would have no impact whatsoever on the peace and the stillness of the love that I feel. There would be no reaction, no response. Stillness would continue its peaceful existence of love, wholly unaffected.

'After some time, I come back to awareness of myself as Aedamar, and awareness of my physical self in the world, understanding that I had been brought beyond my finitude into infinity itself, into being itself, and into love itself. I felt blessed, and awed, and full of love; my being transformed into love.'

DETACHMENT AND LETTING GO

Along with surrender, we also need to cultivate detachment. Meister Eckhart is a master teacher of detachment, which he called 'letting go'. I recommend that everyone explore Meister Eckhart. His teaching is exhilarating, profound and powerful. Eckhart believed that detachment was critical for coming to know God, and for rising into spiritual consciousness. Developing detachment is necessary both in meditation and in ordinary life. It is the ability to let go of egoic concern with worldly things and desires in order to be fully available for God. It is the art of moving beyond expectation, and egoic desires, into pure acceptance both in meditation and in everyday life.

It is not a naive rejection of ordinary life but the ability to be at peace with oneself and others in all that unfolds. Gandhi's great wisdom – 'In order to change the world, change yourself' – is a powerful philosophy of detachment. Detachment is a key part of the shift into higher consciousness. It means to be unconcerned with outcomes, to lose expectations, to be at peace with how things are. Paradoxically, it is radical acceptance of life just as it is.

Being in nature is a powerful way to practise detachment – walking meditatively by the sea, or in the woods, or up a mountain. Letting ourselves be touched by the experience and becoming absorbed into the totality of life, losing all sense of our own identity as separate to the beauty of nature. This gentle feeling, which is so easy to experience in nature, is what we then try to recreate in our ordinary lives.

STAGE THREE: THE LIMINAL SPACE

By developing a practice of meditation, and by learning to surrender and detach, we cross the threshold into unknowing and thereby enter into the liminal space where transformation of consciousness can begin to occur. Moving deeper into this liminal space is precisely the step that is needed for developing our spiritual consciousness.

I described in an earlier chapter my own experience of entering this liminal space on that cold December afternoon, when I went for a walk in the park and a mighty energetic event took place inside me. It happened because I made a conscious decision to surrender to my unusual feelings: to let *them* tell me about themselves; and to let *them* reveal their meaning to me. I let go of my need to know, to name and to explain, and in doing so I made it possible for them tell me something of their nature and meaning. Philosophy had given me the curiosity and the courage to discover more about my mood of detachment, my inexplicable frustration and my metaphysical longing, and so I simply let go.

I will share again a brief summary of the energetics I felt in me that day in the park, to encourage you to open up to the energetics that will be part of your own awakening.

A Lived Experience of the Liminal Space

Once I got to the park I felt a wild energy stir in me, building rapidly in intensity, until I felt that there was an energetic hurricane howling inside me. I resisted nothing. I let it all happen as it wanted to happen, and it was the wildest experience of my life. The energy inside me began telling me to speak, demanding that I give a message, without telling me what to say.

Without the insight I had gained from reading Heidegger, I would most definitely have thought I was losing my mind. And paradoxically, I *was* losing my rational mind. I was taking my first baby steps into higher spiritual consciousness. My awakening had begun.

We must all allow ourselves to be brought into a powerful liminal space, not just as a one-off but as an ongoing attitude. We allow ourselves to be brought into a space beyond our intellectually defined physical universe, a space where different energies operate, a space where knowing is unknowing, where messages are empty, where longing does not seek satisfaction. We must all cross over into the liminal space to discover what the next stage of life holds for us.

It is in this liminal space that the teaching and insights each person needs, in order to become their best self, will be revealed. The gift we receive when we allow ourselves to be brought fully into that liminal space is the gift of our truest and most authentic self.

What I now believe about the energy that urgently asked me to speak that day – telling me to give a message without telling me what to say – is that I was being re-formed by the archetype of the messenger *into* a messenger. And later that evening, when cosmic longing revealed the impossibility of satisfying it, I believe that that was love's longing offering itself to me as the content of the message I was to share. I was becoming a messenger of love. It took me five long years to piece things together in order to understand it in this coherent way.

And by the same measure, every other mystical experience that I have shared in this book also began when I surrendered to the liminal space, when I surrendered myself to God, and allowed myself to be brought out of my body and into communion with the divine presence.

Paradoxically, when we surrender in curiosity and wonder, letting go of the known, a whole new world opens up to us. It is in this liminal space that our consciousness is transformed and our lives begin to be reoriented.

The Consciousness of Longing

> *'The things you desire are seeking you in the same way you are seeking them.'*
> Rumi

Feeling a longing that has no object is totally counterintuitive in our Western capitalist culture of instant gratification. It frustrates us deeply not to be able to map out a linear path to pursue the object of our desire. A longing without an object is alien to us. Yet, it is now critical that we sit with our longing without trying to satisfy it; that we sit in deep curiosity and wonder with this open-ended longing and let *it* tell us what *it* wants in us, for us and of us. We are on the cusp of crossing over into a higher way of knowing and a higher way of being. We are entering spiritual consciousness. We are at the point of no return.

And now something very different happens. In our longing to understand our longing, we slowly realize that it is not our longing at all, but longing itself, expressing itself, in us. The longing we feel is pure longing; it is longing as the natural expression of love. Love has crossed our border, entered us somehow, and most paradoxically of all, it wants nothing except to reveal itself to us. All it wants is our attention, all it wants is for us to engage with it as it is. It simply wants us to know it. It is *calling* us into it. It wants us to be with it and to be one with it. This is revelation. This is exactly what the mystic poet Rumi understood when he said, 'The things you desire are seeking you in the same way you are seeking them.'

This is a major milestone on the path of our spiritual development. One might now be tempted to ask why this is happening – what purpose does it serve? But the whole point is that it is its own purpose; it serves no other purpose than itself. The longing is its own why. Love is its own reason. Meister Eckhart exhorted us to live without a why. Here, at this transformative juncture of our lives, we must now learn to live without a why. And when we do, our finitude is breached, the boundary of our personal consciousness opens to consciousness itself, to the higher realm, to higher knowing, to spirit, to God and to love.

This is the longing that Levinas called 'metaphysical desire' for the great 'Other' of God and he specifically told us that this desire is impossible to satisfy. The paradox is that in remaining unsatisfied, it is in fact satisfied.

It is my deepest belief that by engaging with this longing we are allowing ourselves to be re-formed by the longing of love into the beings of love we are in our original creation. And, beyond even this, we allow ourselves to be guided into the highest meaning and purpose of our life. In other words, we become who we came here to be. My gift was to become a mystic teacher and a messenger of love; another person's gift will be to become the healer, peace-maker, yoga teacher, spiritual leader, doctor, writer or whatever it is their destiny to become. Wherever our most authentic self-expression lies, that is what will open up for us when we surrender to the liminal space of unknowing and to love's longing.

When we follow the lure of this insatiable longing in ourselves, *it* helps us to transcend our finitude; *it* carries us beyond ourselves. Then, quite miraculously, we are able to let go of the finite, transient satisfactions of this material world and let ourselves be drawn into longing's own longing, which wants nothing beyond itself. We let ourselves be drawn into an open-ended relationship with this longing, which is nothing other than God as love. And when we let this happen to us, we realize that love itself has brought us into higher, metaphysical-spiritual, mystical *unknowing.*

STAGE FOUR: MEETING OUR SPIRITUAL MASTERS

A critical stage of our awakening will be to enter a deep and profound spiritual relationship with whatever manifestation of the divine we are drawn to. For me it was Jesus and Mary Magdalene, and then God as love. Awakening is a universal experience that is mediated for each person in their own unique way. Whatever our religion, or faith, or spiritual tradition, our awakening will be guided by the unique manifestation of the divine that is most true to that path. For each of us it will be different: perhaps Jesus, Mother Mary, Mary Magdalene, the female archangels or the ascended masters; or possibly through the teaching of Buddha or a particular mystic or prophet, for example. Our awakening is generally consonant with our faith, tradition or background. It makes sense that we should be in relationship with the particular manifestation of the divine that is most meaningful for us.

TRANSMISSION OF AN AWAKENED MIND

On the human plane, however, an important milestone of the awakening process is to meet or encounter a spiritual teacher whose awakened mind will be transmitted to us, so that our own minds awaken in turn. The old adage that when the pupil is ready, the teacher will appear, is nowhere more true than here. The idea is to be open to recognizing a special spiritual guide coming into our life, just when we need them. I met David through trusting my intuition and following up on the message to go to Séan Boylan's place. When I met David, I knew that something profound had happened to me even though I did not know what it was. It was much later on I understood that, in meeting him, his awakened mind was transmitted to mine.

READING THE MYSTICS

In the West, we probably most often encounter our spiritual teachers and experience this transmission through reading sacred texts, reading the mystics, listening to sacred music and reading books by inspirational spiritual authors. The transmission in this way can be just as powerful as a meeting in person. The list of spiritual writers whose wisdom shaped my awakening mind is too long to share, except to mention in particular Plato, Hildegard of Bingen and Meister Eckhart. Their words, and Hildegard's music, set fire to my soul, igniting my deepest curiosity about what life is really all about. Louise Hay also became one of my teachers in 2015, when I first read *You Can Heal Your Life*. Her writing and wisdom touched me in a very profound way, and it seems nothing short of a miracle that six years later, her company is now publishing this book.

TRANSFORMATION OF CONSCIOUSNESS

Here we are, at the Rubicon of our awakening. The first four stages have prepared the ground, tilled the soil and sowed the seeds. The next three stages will actively orchestrate the transformation of our consciousness. The next three levels of transformation are: unity consciousness; consciousness of the divinity of existence; and union with God.

All that I share here has come from reflecting on the milestones of my own awakening and from my lived experience of these seven stages. I subsequently discovered that my experience followed the path originally mapped out by St Teresa of Ávila, who had also divided her seven stages of awakening into two similar groups. It was affirming to discover that my own categories reflected hers, although she of course offers much greater and deeper teaching about what happens in each 'mansion', as she called them.

STAGE FIVE: UNITY CONSCIOUSNESS

The first level of the transformation of our consciousness is into unity consciousness. Unity consciousness is the felt-awareness in our mind, body and soul of the belonging of everything together in deep and profound connection. It is the higher felt-awareness of the connection of all to All. It is not yet union with the divine, but it is a necessary expansion of our consciousness that is a crucial milestone on the path to mystical consciousness. An example of this is what is commonly described as a 'mountain-top experience' or – as happened to me – a pier-end experience. This was when I first 'got' the incredible connection of all to All. Once again, I stress that this is not a linear path – rather it is fluid, spiralling and unfolding, so I invite you to be open to how this will unfold and flow in your own unique experience.

By letting ourselves be brought into the liminal space, by becoming sensitive to its subtle energies, by becoming still and detached, by letting our minds be awakened, we now open to ever deeper awareness of the inherent connectedness of everything, the belonging of all to All. We are no longer enthralled to the ways of the ordinary world. Instead, we now naturally stand in awe before creation, and so we open fully the depths of our being to the 'mountain-top experience' of living-feeling-knowing the holy connection of all to All. This experience can happen in prayer or in nature or both – when we enter time out of time, and we *feel* and know our belonging to the whole.

Once we have experienced these shifts, we should try to live from this new and higher consciousness.

THE ENERGETICS OF EXPANDED CONSCIOUSNESS

Importantly, our consciousness is actually expanding at an energetic level. This may be experienced as a feeling of 'crossing over', or as an energetic outflow from our bodies, or as a fire burning in us, or a hurricane howling in us, or as an energy coming through us, or in some other way that you may personally experience the expansion. It will be some form of an energetic shift whereby God, light, love dissolves more and more of the boundaries of our finite mind, allowing us to participate more and more in the divine mind. And we *feel* this happening in our energetic field. This is the embodied felt-experience of the transformation of our consciousness.

Imagine the waters of a river arriving at the sea. The river is astonished to be met by seawater that has travelled up into the mouth of the river to welcome the river into its own self. Imagine the river's further joy when it flows into, and becomes one with, the vast expanse of the sea itself. This is what is now happening in us.

We do not understand the experience of our consciousness expanding with our rational mind – we are not meant to! We are now well beyond the rational mind – we are entering the Mind of God. This is a very sacred stage in the process. We are now becoming more spiritual than rational in our awareness, understanding and being. We now engage with the world in a new way. Our frame of reference expands and we feel naturally drawn to include the perspective of love in all that we think, say and do. When we meditate from this consciousness, we open ever deeper to the presence of God.

STAGE SIX: CONSCIOUSNESS OF THE DIVINITY OF EXISTENCE

In time, we become aware of the divinity of all existence. We experience nature and all of life to be shimmering and alive with its divinity. Creation becomes luminous, and an aura of sacredness pervades everything. We sense, feel and somehow know that God is in every created thing, and every created thing is in God. I shared an example of when this first happened to me during the summer solstice walk in 2015. This experience, whether it is a one-off or ongoing, transforms us at our depths, and gives us a whole new insight and understanding of the divinity of creation and of life. We cannot unknow the sacredness of life once we have experienced its divinity. From now on, life itself becomes holy.

TRANSIENT EXPERIENCES

Like all developmental milestones in life, each of these are necessarily transient experiences. We move through them, and we are changed by them. We do not try to hold onto them. Instead, we live through them as transformative experiences that change us at the depths of our being and bring us to the next stage of our development. These experiences I am describing are so deep, profound and powerful that we cannot expect them to be our ongoing state of consciousness – we simply could not live that way. However, we now live out of the awareness of what we have experienced because we live out of our transformed consciousness. It is unrealistic to expect to perceive the divinity of nature all day, every day, but the experiences produce in us a new respect, reverence and awe for and before life. This is the lived experience of the transformation of our consciousness. We soon observe the transformation for the good in ourselves by how we now live our lives.

But this incredible transformation of our consciousness does not stop until we have become one with the One and reached the seventh stage of love.

STAGE SEVEN: MYSTICAL CONSCIOUSNESS; UNION WITH THE DIVINE

Now we approach the highest point of the journey to mature spiritual consciousness. God opens its whole self to us, so that we may immediately (without mediation) experience God as pure, radiant, peaceful, joyous, ecstatic, blazing love. In meditation we are miraculously drawn into divine union and we become one with God. We experience what Julian of Norwich called 'Oneing'. In mystical language, we become God. We can now say, with profound reverence and awe, 'I am The I AM.'

In this glorious and majestic experience of becoming one with God, we undergo the final transformation of our consciousness, and we become what God is: God is love; God is peace; God is justice; God is equality; God is compassion; God is joy; God is the stillness. By knowing God in this way, we are transformed in our own being into what God is. We become God. We share the being of God by embodying these beautiful higher principles of life. At this level of spiritual consciousness, we become the things that we now know.

Another way of describing this is to say: *to know and to understand the higher ideals we must become them.* To understand love, I must become love; and to become love, I must understand it. It is circular. One of the oldest principles of philosophy is that 'like knows like'. Becoming the thing we know is a classic example of that principle: to know love itself, we must somehow become love itself, and this is exactly what happens when we rise to spiritual-mystical consciousness. We become what God is.

Crucially, when we understand these higher ideals with our transformed spiritual consciousness, we instantly feel compelled to act on what we now know, and this is how we will heal our broken world. When I truly understand peace, I become peaceful in my being and then I strive for peace in my own life and in life itself. When I truly understand justice, I become a just person and then I strive for justice in my own life and in life in general. In all this, we become the consciousness of the thing we understand *and we act on it*. We share the consciousness of love, justice, peace, harmony – and we make it our life's work to serve that ideal with our whole being. In my awakening, I came to share the consciousness of love and now I try serve love with my whole life. Each of us will come into the highest calling of our life when we reach this level of consciousness, and then we will naturally, with grace and with ease, dedicate our lives to serving that ideal. Our ideals have become actionable.

When we share the consciousness of love, we become love; we are one with love, and we long to serve love. We become beings of love, beings of peace, beings of justice, beings of equality. We have broken free of the limited structures of human consciousness and have entered the consciousness of *the thing itself*, which is the consciousness of God. We do not want to work for love because our faith tradition tells us it is the right thing to do – we want to work for love because it is now in our nature to work for love, or peace, or whichever ideal draws us to itself. Serving our higher ideal is now the only thing that gives meaning to our lives.

To bring this journey of awakening to its conclusion, I'd like to share the experience I had in one of my most recent meditations, as a lived experience of this pure spiritual consciousness I am trying to describe.

A Lived Experience of Mystical Consciousness

I began the meditation with this prayer: 'Hold me in the embrace of your love, O God, my father, my mother. Hold me forever in the embrace of your love.' Then God replied:

'I hold you forever in the womb of my love. I hold you in the embrace of my love, suckling at the breast of my love. You feed forever on the food of my love, and you need no other food.

'I AM your mother. I AM your father. I AM your brother. I AM your sister. I AM your son. I AM your daughter. I AM your beloved husband. I AM your friend. I AM your enemy. I AM your teacher. I AM your pupil. You are the daughter of my love and I AM your Mother-Father God.

'You have tended to me with your tears and with your love. Only love can understand love. To know me you must love me. Suckle at the breast of my love and I will fill you with my love.

'I AM in everything and everything is in me. I birthed you into my holy womb of my love and you have never left. There is nothing outside my womb. There could be nothing outside my womb. I hold all of creation in the holy womb of my love.

'You are my daughter of love, because you understand my love.'

It is important to say, of course, that engaging with the development of our spiritual consciousness does not mean that everybody's life will take an overtly spiritual turn, as mine did. It just so happened that that was my destiny. What it does mean is that our life is deeply enriched by our coming into the unique expression of who we truly are, whatever that may be – whether as a gardener, for example, or maybe a doctor, sailor, athlete, businessperson, economist, parent, lawyer or politician, perhaps – and through that work we express and live our lives from the higher ideal that now guides our life.

Whatever it is we do, we now do it as an expression of who we are in our truth. We do it in a way that allows us to express and to share our highest actualized self with and in service to the world. It means that we achieve deep meaning, purpose and fulfilment in the area that best allows us to express our unique talents in life. I would have been very happy to be a writer of fiction and a philosopher – life just had something else in store for me when I finally engaged with my awakening.

THE FINAL PARADOX

AWAKENING AS AN EMBODIED EXPERIENCE

The greatest paradox of this whole process of awakening to spiritual consciousness is that it is an embodied experience. What happens in our spirit must happen also in our body. Our awakening is embodied in every cell of our body, in every act, word and thought. Our awakened being becomes who we are in our everyday life. For this reason, it is important to engage in some form of 'body work' to ground our spiritual experiences; whether it be yoga, craniosacral therapy, somatic experiencing, reiki, Tai Chi, spiritual massage, working with essential oils or some other direction, we must allow our bodies to participate in this awakening for it to be a fully integrated experience.

WAKING UP TO LOVE AS THE MEANING OF LIFE

Once it happens, we realize without a doubt that awakening constitutes the whole meaning and purpose of life. By allowing ourselves to be awakened to divine love, we re-embrace the sacred and we learn to co-create our lives with love. This is how we re-spiritualize life, this is how we re-embrace the sacred – by living from the truth that we have come from love and will ultimately return to love.

FROM DIS-EASE TO SPIRITUAL GRACE AND EASE

Thus, it is essential that we identify the feelings of spiritual dis-ease as developmental milestones on the path to spiritual consciousness. They serve a critical role in preparing us for spiritual growth. Without negotiating these highly unusual feelings in a new way, we simply will not experience or achieve mature spiritual growth. Running away from this inner work is running away from who we are.

For too long we have been trying to respond to the archetypal spiritual impulse with things of a different category. But, just as physical hunger cannot be satisfied by psychological empathy, nor can an emotional need be satisfied by a stimulating intellectual discussion, nor can our spiritual needs be satisfied by responding to them with something from a lower category of life.

No amount of logistical planning or intellectual brilliance could ever achieve what is so miraculously achieved when we surrender to our awakening. We did not know the way, but the way was revealed. It works by paradox rather than logic. It works through unknowing rather than knowing. What we learn about ourselves and about life in this way is given to us – we do not achieve it by rational analysis. We receive it through revelation.

When we let ourselves be drawn into transcendental feeling, enquiring into our unusual feelings and opening ourselves to new ways of knowing, our frustration lifts, our dissatisfaction melts away, our emptiness dissolves, our longing subsides, our anxiety ebbs, and we fall desperately and beautifully in love with love itself. We have found what we did not even know we were looking for. The jigsaw pieces of our lives fall into place. With ease, we now know the way to go. The path to follow in our career, our relationships and our life now becomes clear. We are no longer confused about what makes us happy and what gives meaning to our lives. We know now that we are one with the energy of life itself, and so can co-create our highest good with the highest good itself. Meaning and purpose flow into our lives, and we are now fulfilled.

We then look back over the path of our lives, full of breakdown, sadness, pain and trauma, and we realize that all along these were stepping stones to love, directing us onto the track that would give the deepest meaning and the highest purpose to our lives.

~

CONCLUSION

HOPE

'I have come that you may have life,
and have it to the full.'
JESUS, GOSPEL OF JOHN

The great possibility that arises from all that I have shared is hope. Hope comes from accepting that there is no separation; that life is a gift to be enjoyed rather than a punishment to be endured. Hope comes when we accept that waking up to spiritual consciousness is a natural and necessary part of life. It comes from accepting that we are already one with God – light in the light and love in love. It comes when we adopt a new mindset of higher meaning and deeper purpose, rather than struggling in despair and feeling burdened by life.

Once we accept that we are *meant to* enter the light while we still live, then we can have a whole new approach to life. Not to experience the light during our human journey is profoundly to have missed the whole point of life. No longer should spiritual growth be seen as an optional extra that may or may not yield dividends in the next life. Instead, it should be seen as something life-critical and non-negotiable for living this life here and now, as it is meant to be lived. When we do, life will no longer be seen as a struggle for possible gains in the next world, but will instead become completely purposeful and deeply meaningful at the highest possible level, here and now.

Religions all over the world are dying, but people still want God. We are coded and hard-wired for a relationship with a higher power. It is part of our evolutionary make-up to want to know what lies beyond – spiritually as well as materially. This all brings us right up to today – to the 21st century – which finds the world in a state of absolute chaos and potential self-destruction. Our culture is one of rampant consumerism. This beautiful world of ours is crying out in pain. COVID-19; Black Lives Matter marches being met with police brutality; democracies moving towards authoritarianism; fires burning in California and Australia; ice caps melting at the Poles; carbon levels rising as we cut down the Amazon rainforests; even the air we breathe is dependent on nature. Yet, with a profound level of arch stupidity, we hurtle headlong into money-making projects that are killing our planet and that will in turn kill us.

We who pride ourselves on our intellect and all the ways we can use it to make money do so at the expense of the very planet we live on. Where once we were blinded by the brilliance of reason, now we are blinded by greed and stupidity. Both the Earth and her human children are crying in despair and in pain. We are in the last hour – the last minutes. Unless we act now, we lose our exquisitely beautiful home on Mother Earth, and as a species, we become extinct.

It is critical to realize that the spiritual impulse of life did not end when humans mistakenly enthroned reason above spirit. It did not wither away as some unnecessary evolutionary misfit. The spiritual force of life lives on, seeking to express itself despite the fact that we no longer understand it. And just as we humans experience hunger and seek food, or have emotional needs and seek psychological comfort, so too do we experience spiritual hunger. But for too long in the West we have not known how to respond to this hunger, because we did not *know* that what we were feeling was actually spiritual starvation.

Now, however, we must engage with our entirely natural, normal spiritual growth. Spiritual development is a crucial milestone on the path of life, as critical as learning to walk and talk. Failing to learn how to grow spiritually leaves us lost in a very complex world that continues to call us to spiritual engagement.

When we cannot read and interpret the signs, when we have no wisdom to teach us about spiritual growth, we cannot understand the reason for the chaos in our lives. But it is through the breakdowns and the loss of meaning, purpose and direction that the Holy Spirit invites us into spiritual growth. We try to feed our longings with material goods or exciting life experiences, or we may try yoga or mindfulness, but something much more is needed. We need to develop a conscious, mature, open, curious, wise receptivity to the next phase of life, which is our spiritual growth and development.

At this time of human unfolding, spirit, God, life – or whatever name we use – is insisting that we wake up and take action for our spiritual growth as the next ordained stage of human development. When we learn how to interpret the signs of our readiness for spiritual growth, we can then engage with ease in the process of spiritual maturation. The world, which has never *seemed* more sophisticated on the outside, has never *been* more contorted and deformed in its soul.

The amazing news is that humanity is now leaving the Age of Reason. We are once more in an Axial Age. The evolutionary impulse is upon us again and is ushering in a new age: a Spiritual Age, the Age of Love. If humanity had not made these crucial mis-steps in denying and repressing our spiritual needs for 2,000 years, this Spiritual Age would dawn more or less seamlessly as a natural birth process, but this is not happening. The world is not ready for the Spiritual Age because we have neglected to develop our spiritual faculty in any mature and meaningful way. This means that there is a profound mismatch between what the force of life is trying to birth, and our ability to receive and to co-create with it.

Human beings, as ever, are a vehicle through which conscious and intelligent life seeks to express itself. As intelligent beings, we are part of intelligent Being itself. We are designed to co-create life with life, but we have lost the ability to think in any way that is not governed by reason or to value ideas that do not conform with reason.

Since the time of ancient Greek philosophy, some thinkers and mystics have always recognized a level of knowing above rational-intellectual knowing, which is called 'unknowing'. This is where we all need to go now. Unknowing is not irrational; it is supra-rational. It is the knowing of the mystic who has experienced the realm above reason, which is love.

Life, however, is finding it incredibly difficult to bring in this Spiritual Age because we humans are not prepared to receive it, and in our ignorance we are actively blocking it. It is almost alien to us: incomprehensible, meaningless. But the time is now urgently upon us to do everything necessary to grow spiritually so this age is not lost to us and we are not lost to the future of life.

The force of life will express itself – we cannot stop that from happening – but we can fail to receive its riches if we do not quickly develop spiritual practices and intelligence on a par with what life is offering to us.

We are close to the Age of Heaven on Earth, but instead of heralding in this sacred era, we are frantically trying to save our species and Mother Earth from irreversible damage. Love has arrived to find us fighting wars among ourselves and hate dominating the governmental policies of many of our global leaders. The time to act is now. An urgent call has gone out from life itself, from love itself. All hands are needed on deck. It is urgent. The time is now to save ourselves from ourselves, and to save Mother Earth from us.

My life story is a classic testament to the reality of this contorted problem. All along, God, life, the universe was trying to come through to me, offering itself to me as a spiritual unfolding or awakening, but I had no idea what was going on. I was clueless to the signs, the symbols, the nudges of God that the spiritual energy of life itself was trying to welcome me into my highest self-expression. God was offering Its own self to me, and I could make no sense of it.

The dawning of the Spiritual Age is causing profound confusion for humans all over the world, who do not understand these feelings as a natural life event. We have lost the ability to engage with life itself because we have been kept from engaging with our own spiritual growth for more than two millennia.

The wonderful thing, however, is that no human has ever been able to stop the force of life from unfolding according to its own laws. No one could have stopped the big bang, and no one can now stop the momentum and the power of love itself from unfolding for humanity at this time. This is the greatest comfort.

Help is at hand to save humanity and to save Mother Earth. We are slow to understand what is happening because we are so spiritually immature, but life itself is giving crash courses all over the planet to ordinary people like you and me so that we can cooperate in the birthing of this new Spiritual Age of Love.

The life force of the new age is powering in, ready or not, and it is sweeping us all up into its healing energy. In encountering our blocks to it, it is unilaterally elevating us to our highest purpose and our highest living, even though we may not understand what is happening to us. Life is urgently calling to us to cooperate and to join in the revolution of love. Listen, and you will hear the still, quiet voice of God calling to you. Despite how quietly God calls to us individually, the new age *will* topple the old order of non-spiritual existence. It is clearing the way for the unfolding of life itself, which at this time seeks to create heaven on Earth in place of the heart-breaking tragedies strewn across the planet.

The only thing asked of us is to re-embrace the sacred, not as something primitive and regressive, but as something radically post-post-modern, post-post-religious, and radically and eternally life-giving.

In his last book, physicist Stephen Hawking wrote that we have approximately 1,000 years left for viable life on this planet. His advice was to get out of here while we can and to begin 'colonizing' outer space. My advice is to take responsibility for what we have done. Not to run away arrogantly only to do the same elsewhere, but to remain, make reparation, undo the damage, repair, fix, heal and make whole.

And there is one singular means by which all this can be achieved: the radical power of love. Never before in my life have I had such a sense of meaning, purpose, happiness and fulfilment as I have had since I finally understood that I was going through a completely natural life event – a spiritual awakening. Now I am home to myself in my truth and home to myself in God, too. Now I know there is no difference between what I am and what God is; between what you are and what God is; between what you are and what I am. We are created out of the divine substance that is love, and together, we are One.

And so, I pray now, to return to the place I never left, the womb of Christ, the womb of my Mother, Love.

> *'Tell my friends I am waiting patiently for their love, that I am on fire with love for them, as I am on fire with love for you. Invite them to become kindling in the fire of my love so that all may burn together, as one, in Love.'*
>
> JESUS

RESOURCES

ONLINE RESOURCES

Allison Cooke, spiritual artist (lightvibrations.art@gmail.com)
Talented artist who created the beautiful mandala that graces
this book

Cate Gongos (soulseekersjourney.com)
Supports women to connect with who they really are and to
discover the power of their soul

Center for Action and Contemplation (cac.org)
Committed to promoting the Christian contemplative tradition
and helping people experience its transformative wisdom

Claire Zammit (femininepower.com)
Offers a framework, principles and practices designed to help
women realize their full potential and contribute their gifts at
the highest level

John O'Donohue (johnodonohue.com)
Late Irish poet-philosopher and author

The Eckhart Society (eckhartsociety.org)
Dedicated to the study and promotion of the principles and teachings of Meister Eckhart, a medieval theologian, philosopher and mystic

On Being Studios (onbeing.org)
Pursuing deep thinking and moral imagination, social courage and joy, to renew inner life, outer life and life together

FURTHER READING

108 Mystics: The Essential Guide to Seers, Saints and Sages, Carl McColman (Hay House, 2017)

Anam Cara: Spiritual Wisdom from the Celtic World, John O'Donohue (Bantam, 1999)

'Arise, My Love...': Mysticism for a New Era, William Johnston (Orbis, 2000)

Divine Beauty: The Invisible Embrace, John O'Donohue (Bantam, 2004)

Eternal Echoes: Exploring our Hunger to Belong, John O'Donohue (Bantam, 2000)

Light is the New Black: A Guide to Answering Your Soul's Callings and Working Your Light, Rebecca Campbell (Hay House, 2015)

Many Lives, Many Masters: The true story of a prominent psychiatrist, his young patient and the past-life therapy that changed both their lives, Dr Brian Weiss (Little, Brown, 1994)

Selected Writings, Meister Eckhart, ed. Oliver Davies (Penguin, 1994)

The Mystical Thought of Meister Eckhart: The Man from Whom God Hid Nothing, Bernard McGinn (Crossroad Publishing, 2001)

Mysticism: A Study in the Nature and Development of Spiritual Consciousness, Evelyn Underhill (first published 1911; reprinted E.P. Dutton and Co., 1930; reprinted Dover Publications, 2003)

Mysticism in English Literature, Caroline F.E. Spurgeon (first published Cambridge University Press, Cambridge, 1913; reprinted The Echo Library, 2006)

The Origins of the Christian Mystical Tradition: From Plato to Denys, Andrew Louth (Oxford University Press, 2007)

Phenomenology and Mysticism: The Verticality of Religious Experience, Anthony J. Steinbock (Indiana University Press, 2007)

Scivias, Hildegard of Bingen, transl. Mother Columbia Hart (Paulist Press, 1990)

The Symposium, Plato, transl. Walter Hamilton (Penguin, 1951)

Trials of a Visionary Mind: Spiritual Emergency and the Renewal Process, John Weir Perry (State University of New York Press, 1999)

The Universal Christ: How a Forgotten Reality Can Change Everything We See, Hope For and Believe, Richard Rohr (SPCK Publishing, 2019)

The Way of the Rose: The Radical Path of the Divine Feminine Hidden in the Rosary, Clark Strand and Perdita Finn (Random House USA, 2019)

LISTENING

Meister Eckhart's Living Wisdom: Indestructible Joy and the Path of Letting Go, Jim Finley (Sounds True, 2015)

O Virtus Sapientiae, Hildegard of Bingen, *Early Music*, Kronos Quartet (Nonesuch, 1997)

Saint Hildegard of Bingen: A Feather on the Breath of God, Gothic Voices (Hyperion, 1985)

The Origin of Fire: Music and Visions of Hildegard von Bingen, Anonymous 4 (Harmonia Mundi, 2005)

Tondal's Vision, Ensemble Dialogos (Édition Arcana, 2003)

ACKNOWLEDGEMENTS
AND THANKS

M y deepest thanks to my precious husband, Declan Doyle, whose friendship, love and kindness I could not live without. To my beautiful children, Laragh and Cuan, who give meaning to my life, whose love, company and conversation I treasure. I love you both with all of my heart.

My childhood friends Bronagh, Jenny, Joy and Riona, whose love and riotous good company uplifts and enriches my life. My friend Laura, one of most loving and authentic souls I know. My incomparable and wonderful sisters, Richelle, Keelin, Melrona, Muireann – thank you for your love and support – and especially Evana, who is a constant source of loving, encouraging, fun and wise sisterly love. My beautiful brother, James, a kindred spirit on the path of life. Gerardo Gutierrez, whom I met when doing an internship in Chicago 30 years ago and whose friendship still lights me up. Maurita Moore, a companion of my soul. Eleanor Dawson, friend and wise guide on the spiritual path. Jeannette Marsh, for inspiring and soulful conversations. Dea Bozzo and

Sasha Padron, whose friendship I will carry with me for life and beyond. Tricia Bird, a blessing in my life. Cate Gongos, with whom it is a joy to walk the spiritual path. Elizabeth Ellis, a soul friend and a writing companion. Paula Knox, who generously and with grace helped me out with school runs and took Cuan home many times when I had deadlines to meet for college essays. Claire Zammit of Feminine Power, whose wise mentoring and phenomenal teaching helped me to understand and contextualize my mystical experiences as part of the evolutionary unfolding of life in our time. Jean Houston, whose teaching modelled courage-in-action to live as a mystic in co-creation with life itself. Brian Peoples, whose spiritual friendship, care and support has been a guiding light in my life; without your help I would still be lost. I am deeply grateful. Allison Cooke, more angel than human, whose soul-friendship has sustained me on the spiritual journey, and who channelled the exquisite mandala 'Channel of Divine Love' on the cover of this book – grateful to have met you (again). Eileen Elizabeth Heneghan, whose wise guidance has been invaluable to me. Siobhan Byrne and Emma Fraser, whose loving friendship is a gift to me. Elizabeth and Eoin, whose company and conversation are always a pleasure and a joy. Michael and Diane, for your generous friendship. My godmother, Nancy, who nurtured my early love of reading with an illustrated book of Hans Christian Andersen fairy tales that lit a spark of magic in my imagination. My aunt Mairead for her incredible generosity and love. Aunts Carmel, Moira, Pauline, Bríd, and Uncle Padraic, for their love and support. All of my in-laws and brilliant nieces and nephews – too many to name. Father David Weakliam, for his beautiful friendship. Karen and

Conor, whose warm-hearted and inspiring company is a joy in my life. Phil Kearney-Byrne, an instant soul friend when we met on the MA in creative writing – her easy laughter, and her wise, intelligent and challenging conversations are among the best in my life. Anne Enright, for her teaching on the MA in creative writing, and for believing in the radically postmodern novel I was writing. Poet Paula Meehan, whose wise guidance and teaching on the MA opened me up to the subtle working and nuance of depth creativity. She taught me how to scry for the poem or the story that wants to come through me, like a diviner: intuiting, sensing, feeling and channelling it, so that I learned how to let the words almost write themselves onto the pages of my books. In many ways she uniquely prepared me for writing this book. To Nirmala Nataraj, for her wonderful and incisive editing eye. To Michelle Pilley and the team at Hay House UK, for their warm welcome to the Hay House family. Finally, my most sincere thanks to Emily Arbis and Stephanie Farrow, whose excellent editorial support helped to make this a far better book than it would have been had it been left to my efforts alone. Any remaining failings are of course my own.

ABOUT THE AUTHOR

Aoife Herrity

Aedamar Kirrane lived a conventional life with an unconventional soul until the age of 46 when her spontaneous awakening helped her realize she was never meant to fit into a world that denied the need for mature spiritual development.

Becoming a mother to her two wonderful children was the catalyst that reoriented her life towards its true North Star.

The move from law to philosophy and creative writing was the path by which she came into her truth and to the brink of her awakening.

Aedamar feels most at home at the edge of the Atlantic Ocean in the west of Ireland because it recreates her true sense of belonging between two worlds.

www.aedamarkirrane.com

HAY HOUSE

Look within

Join the conversation about latest products,
events, exclusive offers and more.

f Hay House

🐦 @HayHouseUK

📷 @hayhouseuk

💜 healyourlife.com

We'd love to hear from you!